micro
architecture

richard horden

lightweight,
mobile
and
ecological
buildings
for
the
future

micro
architecture

With 680 illustrations.

Thames & Hudson

concept	Richard Horden
	Ulrike Fuchs
editing	Richard Horden
	Ulrike Fuchs
	Burkhard Franke
layout	Ulrike Fuchs
text	Richard Horden
	Phyllis Richardson
translation + proofreading	Richard Horden
	Lisa Cutmore
	Phyllis Richardson
	Burkhard Franke
	Ulrike Fuchs
	Poppy Horden
	Julia Jakubicka
production	Grafik und Druck GmBH, Munich

On the cover:
Image by Simone Hiesinger, Michael Kehr,
Eike Schling and Sandra Spindler.

First published in the United Kingdom in 2008 by
Thames & Hudson Ltd, 181A High Holborn,
London WC1V 7QX

www.thamesandhudson.com

British Library Cataloguing-in-Publication Data
A catalogue record for this book is available from
the British Library

ISBN: 978-0-500-34249-7

Printed and bound in Germany

contents

micro architecture

Tales of weightlessness and wonder Munich is a city touched by the grandeur of the Alps and by the technological achievements of the twenty-first century. Marked also by an architectural heritage that includes the birth of the Blauereiter movement at Murnau on Lake Staffelsee with Wassily Kandinsky, Franz Marc and others in 1911 and the revolutionary designs of the 1972 Olympic Park, it continues to be graced by groundbreaking, internationally acclaimed structures, like the Allianz Stadium (Herzog and de Meuron), the award-winning airport (Murphy/ Jahn and Koch und Partner) and lately Coop Himmelb(l)au's BMW 'World', which really does pose questions about current approaches to our own built world. Posing more such questions is a professor who leads an architecture programme here that has gained international attention and wide appeal for its achievements in small designs. Inspired by Case Study Houses and nautical and aviation design, Richard Horden leads students to produce built projects that

aerial photograph of munich

MP

demonstrate the latest and most revolutionary heights of structural and material development on the micro level, somewhere between architecture and industrial design.

High-tech Lessons from Nature The first surprise about this work, then, is the explanation that many of the design ideas are taken almost directly from nature, from the penguin that has withstood eons of subzero temperatures and blasting gales, to the sturdy reed and humble duck. As nature has endowed flora and fauna with the most efficient equipment for surviving in their environments, students at TUM, before putting pen to paper (or fingertips to keys) take a long, hard look at how the expert – nature – functions in specific conditions for clues. To this research are added site visits, which are an adventure in themselves, such as a recent trip to Greenland organized as part of a project with students and professors from the Danish

RH   RH

Technical University in Copenhagen to develop a small-scale ice camp for overnight stays. After flying in, the team will travel to their remote destination by dog sled. Studies of ducks were used to inform the design of a boat paddled by means of a cross-trainer taken directly from the gym. As Horden explains, 'Ducks don't swim backwards, why should you sit backwards to row a boat?' At a larger, planetary scale, our experience of 'nature' in orbit is not so easy to observe, so research into the creation of an astronaut workstation developed at TUM by Hans Huber with Professor Eduard Igenbergs, with seat restraint and folding desk added by team RH, as well as a space shower and sleeping suit, involved sending students in parabolic flights conducted by NASA technicians to test the use of the prototypes in microgravity. The second surprise about the TUM's programme is that many of these research projects get built. This is a programme that wants to see ideas thought through to the last bolt. It may not mean that every

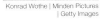
Konrad Wothe | Minden Pictures | Getty Images

RH

RH

idea is produced at 1:1 scale, but this is a place where a lot of model-making happens, a lot of research into new materials (as well as site, climate, topography) and then often, at the very least, a workable prototype that elicits outside interest and/or funding for real-size structures.

Framing a Vision Richard Horden studied at the Architectural Association. Having lived near the sea, he became interested in new materials and building methods used to make stronger, faster ocean craft and was keen to explore new materials in his studies. But, in the AA of the 1960s, much to his consternation, he was directed to build in concrete, which he found too heavy and monumental for the kind of buildings he was interested in creating. Having discovered the Case Study Houses and the work of Eliot Noyes and Craig Ellwood in California, Horden felt those structurally elegant buildings 'confirmed what I'd always felt', a marriage of 'nature

RH

BB

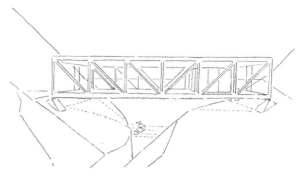

and man' that stirred the inspiration for more nature-centred forms. Being less about density of material and more about being open to the outdoors, these were designs in which glass and transparency figured heavily.

All of these characteristics are evident in Horden's design for his first project, a house for his parents in Poole. Typically for Horden, the design went against the grain of what was being taught during his years in architecture school, and he received a rather discouraging crit when he presented the house as his diploma project in 1973. Horden later built his 'Courtyard House', which he describes as 'a modular structure, that was efficient and easy to build', despite its complex geometries of 4-way and 6-way joints. His mother still lives in the house, and it was designated a Grade II-listed building in England in 2007.

JD

HD

The leap from Case Study House to micro architecture 'is easy', says the architect. 'Ellwood's Mountain House shows the frame structure that should have become prevalent over masonry in subsequent decades but didn't, though many masonry buildings are actually frame structures underneath.' But it was a while before his scaled down approach could be put into practice. As Horden watched the postmodernists of the 1980s reaching back even further for references and eschewing frame for masonry or simply using both, he bided his time and believed that lightweight, modular structures would eventually see the light of day, if not the pages of the architectural press. But he didn't have to wait long before his contribution to the field was to be recognized.

In 1973 Horden was part of the team (with Jan Kaplicky of Future Systems) at Spence & Webster who won the competition to design the new Parliamentary Building in London, a fine achievement for a young, newly qualified architect. From there he went on to a highly fruitful working experience at Foster and Partners. Working on such projects as the Sainsbury Centre, the HongKong Shanghai Bank, Stansted Airport and an all-aluminium house for Norman and Wendy Foster with engineer Tony Hunt, which was developed through to planning permission but sadly never built, energized Horden's instinct for innovation and his belief in frame structure.

When Richard Horden left his long tenure with Foster and Partners, it wasn't because of a clash of egos, but simply because of his desire to pursue his own vision of architecture. Horden remains an admirer of both Foster the man and his work, often citing moments in his time there with glowing enthusiasm, particularly the site visits by helicopter, a machine that he continues to find fascinating and inspiring in very practical terms. Having built the 'Yacht House' in 1983 (which, he says, was influenced by the Sainsbury Centre), he founded his own practice in 1985.

Today, Horden maintains his London practice, now Horden Cherry Lee, which continues to win competitions and produce outstanding buildings in the UK and abroad, including a recent design for a 45-storey office building in London's Docklands, inspired by water plants and using foundations that mimic a reed structure, like the pilings used for hundreds of years in that inimical city built on water, Venice.

Lessons Learned and Taught But nature is one component of the design process. 'The primary teaching goal here is to understand architecture through the frame system,' Horden says of his programme at the TUM. But this is not an end in itself. 'The frame structure has transparency, and it can be lightweight, mobile and in some cases, like the Farnsworth House or Mies and Philip Johnson's Seagram Building, even made to look frameless.' Inspired by modernism in its true meaning, using pure frame structure and the most advanced materials in the best way possible, Horden passes on a love of pure forms and their efficiency learned through his own experience, in conjunction with an abiding respect for the natural environment. Horden's interest in frame structures has led to the development of virtually every project developed at the TUM that strives to minimize the demands on or disturbance of the site. To 'touch the earth lightly', an axiom originating from Australian architect Glenn Murcutt, has inspired a generation of architects to rethink the very foundation of their buildings, how they meet the ground and what impact they have there. It is a theme with which Horden's students have become familiar over the course of their studies, where they learn to question every ounce of building material, every sliver of supporting structure: the joins in the 'Point Lookout' and 'Beach Point', for example, the anchor-points for the 'Ski Haus', the placement of work surfaces, window open-

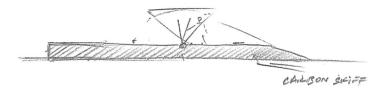

CARBON SKIFF

ings and fixtures in the 'micro compact home' and the design of the very tables that students use for presentations. Adding to the rigorous investigations of structure, the students closely study materials and context. That is, they are made aware not only of the advances in material but in the limited period we might have in which to use them in a particular way, that we build in an evolving continuum, and that the structures we produce necessarily reflect the age and its technical capabilities. Aluminium is favoured for its lightweight strength and its lack of 'off-gassing', release of potentially toxic chemicals, which is vitally important when designing for the contained, fragile atmosphere of space vehicles. But, as Horden puts it, our use of aluminium may have to end at some unforeseen point, so we have to use it well now and be able to adapt when the next challenge comes along. Carbon fibre is also being explored for the current paddle boat project because of its light weight and strength. Though Horden and his team are well aware of the environmental costs in producing the material, they continue to weigh those costs against the efficiency of building with something that gives so much strength and support in such a small mass of material. The pluses may never outweigh the environmental losses for this particular fibre, but the testing and the experimenting may prove a breakthrough in some areas where carbon fibre is the only appropriate substance. Or the methodology, the undaunted spirit of trial and error may prove revolutionary with some new material. The point is to keep looking for what works best. TUM students spend a lot of time in factories overseeing the fabrication of components and prototypes until they either get what they want or become an expert in what doesn't work, valuable training in any field.

I first became acquainted with Richard Horden's programme when I came across TUM's 'Ski Haus' and 'Fish Haus', which I included in *XS: Big Ideas, Small Buildings* as terrific examples

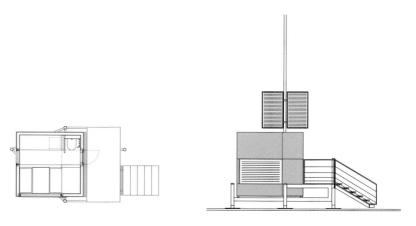

of mobile designs that use 'crossover' technologies (such as in aviation and boat design) to maximize efficiency in material, energy use and space. The next volume, *XS Green*, included the 'micro compact home' because it had been designed to do so many of the things that a genuinely environmentally friendly project should and to the minimum scale necessary to meet basic (as well as very high-tech) living requirements. Happily, the upcoming volume *XS Extreme* will include the Antarctic Pods for the German research team and 'Peak Lab'. These are fine examples of the way Richard Horden has encouraged his students to reach beyond the demands of everyday building, by challenging them to attack the challenges of extreme climate and location and make buildings that are the equivalent of a skilled, well-trained mountaineer. I find it telling, in fact, that whereas Le Corbusier in the 1920s described a house as a 'machine for living', Horden and his students refer to their 'micro compact home' as 'an instrument for

RH

LC   FP

living'. While the former term has the ring of a powered entity that might well run without (or over) the inhabitant, 'instrument' suggests something smaller, more agile and totally within the control of the user. Even though Richard Horden may have taken his cue from the Case Study Houses and modular building, his vision has been more ambitious, to create structures that can function not only in temperate zones like California, but in the most difficult conditions on earth. As demands on the planet and its finite resources confront designers of all-size structures in every location with an ecological imperative, the ability to work comfortably and dynamically within limits – of size, material, energy – will become not only an increasingly marketable skill but an invaluable one. Richard Horden has shaped, with his students and teaching team, the beginnings of what has come to be called micro architecture, in which all of the necessary elements of a building are brought down to their minimum size for maximum use and efficiency. Though it is a term that sounds as if it has been around a long time (and in Horden's mind it has), in actual fact, with reference to architecture, it has yet to be fully recognized or officially defined. Richard Horden cites Le Corbusier's *Cabanon*, or shed, on the Côte d'Azur (1952) and Norman Foster's Cockpit in Cornwall (1962) as early examples of what one might call 'micro architecture', and it is easy to find both the compact design of the *Cabanon* and the transparency of Foster's early 'minimal glass bubble', as he called it, in the projects that students of the TUM have produced under Horden's guidance. But these are only the starting points for designs that continue to question how much of what we build is really necessary or qualifies as best possible practice. And it is no mean feat to be at the beginning of such things, even in small quantities, bolstered by a vision of greater things to come.

phyllis richardson

micro architecture | introduction

This book is dedicated to my dear mother, Irene, now 92, whose support, understanding and acute visual awareness has enhanced all the projects here. She commissioned my first project the 'Courtyard House' in 1972, where she lives today and encouraged me to buy the land on Poole Harbour where my daughter, Poppy, and I now live and share weekends together.

● SAAB

● VOLVO

● DTU

● LOTUS
● ASTON MARTIN
● ROLLS ROYCE
● MINI   LONDON   ● AMSTERDAM
● MCLAREN   ● EADS   ● VW
POOLE   ● TUD

● SMART
● THYSSENKRUPP
● ERCO   ● ZEISS

● DIOR   ● OPEL
● RENAULT   ● SKODA
● YSL   ● PUMA
PARIS   ● ADDIDAS
● CHANEL   ● VEUVE CLICQUOT
● CHARTIER
● CITROEN   ● PORSCHE   ● AUDI
● PEUGEOT   ● MERCEDES
● ESA
                      ● BMW   ● micro compact home
                      ● MUNICH
● IWC   ● ETH   ● TUM   ● HEAD
● SWATCH ● ZÜRICH   ● ZUMTOBEL
          ● ITR ● NESPRESSO
              ● NESTLE
              HTA
              HTW
          ● ZERMATT
ski haus ● ● PRADA   ● BUGATTI
● MIUMIU   ● D&G   ● ILLY
          ● GUCCI ● RIVA
● FIAT ● VERSACE   ● VENICE
● ALFA ROMEO
● AIRBUS   ● WALLY
                          ● MASERATI
● WALLY   ● LAMBORGHINI
                          ● FERRARI
● SEAT
● CUSTO
                          ● BULGARI

introduction

What better place to write about micro architecture than overlooking Lake Zurich? There's a view of the Uetliberg with it's slim mast high above the city on my right, the lush grass and forest hillsides of the Hirzel protected landscape directly across the lake, Mount Rigi above Lucerne and the white sculptural crags of the Titlis and Glarus mountains to the left. It is a happy accident of the deadline for the MoMA exhibition and flight schedules that I am here, an enforced moment of silence in a location of such beauty, a reminder that ideas for micro architecture come first from forms in nature, like the Alps.

This book is composed of two parts, the duality that makes up an architect's life: studio and projects, concepts and reality, mind and material.

RH

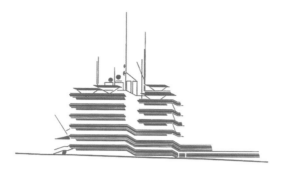

Firstly, I want to say something about how I came to micro architecture and to Munich and how the two inspirations – design philosophy and sense of place – have merged in my work and that of students I lead at the TUM. In 1991 we, the team at my office in London (then Richard Horden Associates), had been involved in the design of some large buildings in England, in particular the Queen's Stand at Epsom Racecourse. The project had to be built to a very tight programme and the work could not be allowed to interrupt any of the horse racing events, in particular the Derby, one of the most important races in the international equestrian calendar. The existing building had to be demolished and a new facility built for 5,000 champagne-sipping race-goers. It was to include tiered viewing terraces, private boxes, jockey changing and weighing rooms, bars, a cinema and restaurants as well as the Queen's private rooms and dining room. The pressure to deliver the project efficiently was even more acute than usual as Queen

this page:
'Queen's Stand'

opposite page:
Her Majesty The
Queen at the
'Queen's Stand',
Epsom

DG   DG

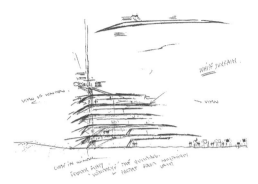

Elizabeth II and members of the royal family attend events here every year and any delay might affect their accommodation.

One of the surest ways to achieve a fast build is to construct components off site and to reduce the problems on site as much as possible to a simple assembly process. For this reason, we decided that all of the balconies and roof elements would be prefabricated. The inspiration for those elements was near at hand. I was fascinated by the petite character of the oldest structure on the course, the Prince's Stand, which is located just to the west of the site for the new building. The relatively small and delicate-looking balcony and canopy of this charming Edwardian building had, I felt, a perfect scale that should be echoed in the new building. We presented the design drawings, models and mock-ups to the Queen in the Picture Gallery at Buckingham Palace in 1990.

RH

DG

micro architecture | 23

To make the prefabricated roof canopies we engaged a specialist aluminium factory that normally produces aviation components. As a designer I enjoyed the regular visits to the factory to check the balcony detailing, quality and progress. We used other manufacturers for the roof canopies, the television interview point, even the mahogany handrail for the Queen's balcony. This practice of engaging a specific 'crossover' manufacturer to prefabricate elements for assembly of discreet portions of the design seemed to me a delightful way to build. The idea of reducing the building elements to a minimum proved very effective and the project was completed after only four months of on-site construction in time for Derby Day 1993, and for a very happy client!

this page:
Italian fishing rig;
interview point at
the 'Queen's Stand',
Epsom

opposite page:
'Point Lookout'
on Fraser Island;
'micro compact home'

LD'A

RH

In my mind 'micro architecture' was born then, and not only as an effective and fast building method but as a teaching tool to help young architectural students to design and manage their own projects. In fact, the press and television interview point on the Queen's Stand directly influenced the 'Point Lookout' project in Australia, as well as canopies we later designed for Buckingham Palace and other viewpoint projects developed with my students at the TU Munich (where I began teaching in 1996), which we now refer to as 'micro architecture'. Ten years later we developed the 'micro compact home', which I view as a direct descendent of the Queen's Stand balconies. This time, however, complete delivery of the building to the site is accomplished in five minutes!

RH

SK

prof. richard horden **introduction**

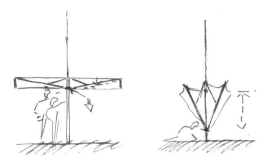

The 'architecture simulator' My first opportunity to teach 'micro architecture' came later in 1991 when Peter McLeary of the Graduate School of Architecture at the University of Pennsylvania called with an invitation for me to lead a guest teaching programme over two terms. I had established a small office in central London with a good foundation of work so the possibility of taking time out to teach for a series of short visits to Philadelphia was appealing. We had won several major international competitions since being awarded the commission for a new Parliamentary Building at Westminster 1974 for Spence & Webster. I had also spent ten hard-working and highly informative years at Foster Associates before starting my own office. So by the time the opportunity at the University of Pennsylvania came up, I had been nurturing a real desire to develop some experimental ideas, essentially to find a way to bring the experience and intensity of an international practice directly to students.

this page and
opposite:
'Folding Canopies' for
Buckingham Palace

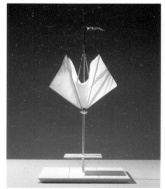
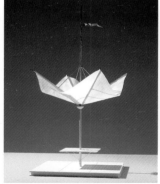
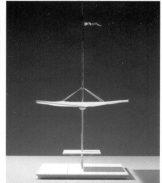

EO

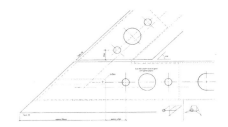

I had admired the way that Craig Ellwood had worked and built with students from UCLA and the Art Centre College on the Bridge House and other projects in the 1960s. The task as I saw it was to condense modern architectural theory, practice and building into a two-semester programme. This could only be done with small-scale projects, a kind of 'architecture simulator'. Flying in on the approach to JFK and Philadelphia in the cockpit of a 747 with a friend, Captain Mauleverer, I was inspired by the landscape of forests and rivers, inlets and islands. As a result, the first project we set for the students was for a compact rugged retreat that could be installed by truck or a light helicopter. A primary task in 'micro architecture' teaching is to engage with the students to achieve 'less material and more nature'. Students have to select their own sites – in this case an area on Whissahikon Creek on the outer west side of the city – and then develop a project that epitomizes their particular chosen landscape and natural light.

EO

RH

MUNCHENER
'DACH SPINNE'

'FLUSS SPINNE'

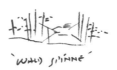

'WALD SPINNE'

CAPRI...
'WAND SPINNE'
(NAPOLI)

After the first-term presentations, students teamed up to build and install a selected short-list of designs on the sites. One of these was a light fishing platform that could be lifted into place at various locations. We called the project 'Flying Water' and it gave the graduate students a full, if high-speed, experience and insight into the process of design, construction and installation, as well as exposing them to the potential problems of a full-scale, proof-of-concept prototype, for the project that was to follow.

Two graduate students who were part of the 'Flying Water' project, Ken Boyd and Brian Kelly, came to work in our office in London, where they focused intensively for three months on the design and construction of the 'Ski Haus'. They then worked in the yacht factory at Sparcraft in Lymington in the New Forest close to Poole, where they supervised the construction and assembly and helped to translate the drawings into the complex geometry, 3D, 8-mm

this page:
'Flying Water'

opposite page:
Ken Boyd and Brian
Kelly at the 'Ski Haus';
a Rutan VariEze

RH

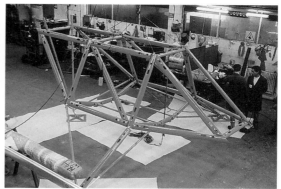

KB

'BERG WALD SPINNE'

'WIENER FISCH SPINNE'
---- MÖRZER SPINNE

'BERG SPINNE'

ZERSTÖRT
BERGFÜHRER
SPINNE'

plate-jointing system. The 'Ski Haus' was significant in that it offered the students the chance to participate in the full design process, from sketches to factory construction and delivery to Switzerland. Completed in 1991, the 'Ski Haus' project was closely followed by 'Point Lookout' in Australia (for students in Adelaide in 1992) and the canopies for Buckingham Palace in 1993.

Today the same principles underlie our teaching programme at the TU Munich, although technology has moved on and with it demands for reduced energy and CO_2 emissions as well as material reduction. The popular inspiration for micro design has also evolved from structures like the hang-glider to ever more compact models of mobile phones and laptop computers and even to emerging designs in lightweight, compact space travel, such as the VariEze aircraft developed by Burt Rutan, and the Virgin Galactic space shuttle.

AK

RH

Andreas Vogler Following a lecture at the Rhode Island School of Design in 1994, I was approached by a Swiss student who was doing his year out at RISD, Andreas Vogler. He was extremely enthusiastic and, being the head of the student union at the Eidgenossische Technische Hochschule (ETH) Zurich, he invited me to fly the 'Ski Haus' from the Berner Oberland (where it was being used for short stays by ski touring and mountaineering groups) for a lecture and exhibition at the ETH. He had created an excellent mountain-top modular project, and we became good friends, as we both enjoyed discussing the potential innovations that could be achieved while teaching and developing micro architecture together with students in the environment of the Swiss Alps.

In 1995 I was invited to teach a short programme at the TU Vienna. Andreas joined me and we embarked on the first of many micro-architecture projects together. The most notable

this page:
Andreas Vogler;
'Fish Haus'

CH

of these was produced by a very energetic and talented group of nine Viennese students led by Brigitte Kunsch and her now husband, Gerhard Abel. It was a car-top cabin project then known as 'Fish Haus' built in carbon fibre. We now refer to the project as the 'Audi Haus' as it is designed to fit above an Audi A3.

After giving a lecture at the TU Munich, I was offered a post as professor in the architecture department and asked Andreas to join me. I was happy to be allowed and encouraged to maintain my London office while teaching part of the week in Munich. Andreas and I began teaching micro architecture at TU Munich in November 1996. I had inherited a team of five teaching assistants from the previous professor and Andreas helped enormously with guiding the team in the initial stages of micro architecture as well as guiding my persistently halting German! However, to my surprise, lectures and teaching in English were encouraged at the university, as a facility with the language would be an advantage to the students in the international job market. We enjoyed being with the students on a weekly basis, though I learned that at the time it was unusual for most German professors to be seen so often by the students. They seemed to live on another plane. However, we, the students and teaching staff, all found studio work at the desk (*zu tisch*) to be tremendously rewarding and inspirational, and the projects developed with the students, for example 'Beach Point' and 'Cliffhanger', demonstrated the great potential for innovation in this environment.

prof. richard horden

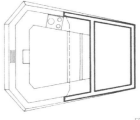

FP

Inspired towards micro architecture It is most important to understand that the foundation of micro architecture is not in architecture at all. Other than the experimental *Cabanon* by Le Corbusier at Cap Martin and the Cockpit at Creak Vean by Norman and Wendy Foster, you could not, at the time we began teaching, find many examples of this type of building in books or magazines. The foundation was then, and still is, nature itself. Munich, with its proximity to the Alps, lakes, forests, mountains steep gorges and meandering rivers, makes for an extraordinarily rich mix of inspiration that is evident in the variety of resulting projects. From the aerodynamic shape of the car-top cabin (informed by the fluid dynamics of the fish), to the cliff-hanging form of the recent 'Peak Lab' and of course the self-contained habitation of the micro compact home, the climate and immediate natural surroundings have contributed to the many wonderful ideas that continue to emerge from the students' projects. We also draw on nature

this page:
Cabanon, Le
Corbusier;
Cockpit, Sir Norman
Foster and Wendy
Foster

opposite page:
'micro compact home',
interior

LC

FP

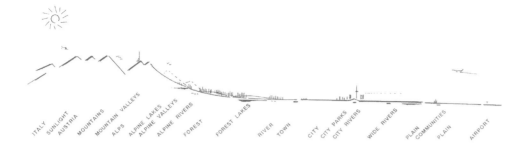

ITALY SUNLIGHT AUSTRIA MOUNTAINS MOUNTAIN VALLEYS ALPS ALPINE LAKES ALPINE VALLEYS ALPINE RIVERS FOREST FOREST LAKES RIVER TOWN CITY CITY PARKS CITY RIVERS WIDE RIVERS PLAIN COMMUNITIES PLAIN AIRPORT

well beyond the mountains. Our projects for extreme environments learn from the forms and biology of the vegetation or creatures that inhabit that extreme place: penguins in the antarctic, lizards in the desert, ducks on the lake and lagoons, reeds by the polder, maritime pines in the high wind Atlantic coasts, palm trees that survive tsunamis!

The city of Munich also enhances the programme through its urban makeup. Munich has a small and sophisticated population of one million and the benefit of a very high level of production skill in local industries of international renown, such as aerospace (Deutsche Aerospace and Kaiser Traide), car production (BMW, and Audi at Ingolstadt), computing (Siemens), interiors (Bulthaup), and lighting technology for the film industry (ARRI). Culturally and creatively we also gain from being near to the Frauenhoffer Institute for environmental design and the offices of *Detail* magazine, the highest circulation architectural magazine worldwide.

DG

* TRADITIONAL CHALET.   STORAGE OF EQUIPMENT ON SIDES AND BELOW OVERHANG.   * SKI HAUS.   SPACE BELOW THE HOUSE ....   * EARLY HIGH ZERMATT MOUSEY STORE?

Nature inspires micro architecture not only through form but through our awareness of the need for conservation of land and resources. **'Touch the earth lightly'**, an aboriginal philosophy that was brought into architectural parlance by Australian architect Glenn Murcutt, has become a much-used phrase. However, it has a particular relevance for our micro architecture projects and helps promote a better understanding and appreciation in our students for nature and whatever site they may be working with – flat ground, hillside and mountain – as well as less obvious characteristics such as the landfall, the tactile and textural quality of the ground surface in both detail and distance. Today 'touching the earth lightly' also refers to energy efficiency and carbon reduction. So the perfect micro architecture project enhances its natural setting and makes the least disturbance to nature, at the same time consuming less energy and the least carbon in its production.

this page:
Child learning
to climb;
grain hut

opposite page:
'St. Louis Arch',
Eero Saarinen

HG

BF

Zwishchen Though we take a great deal of inspiration from nature, we also look to other areas of production and technology to help us achieve the best combination of form and function. *Zwishchen* is a German word meaning 'between' and pronounced 'swischen' like swish, it sounds fast! I enjoy the word and we use it to encourage research for projects that exist between things: often important innovations are found by the combination of two seemingly separate objects. The 'Ski Haus' combines helicopter technology with the traditional Zermatt mountain hut or grain store; the 'TU_FiN' boat brings the exercise machine out of the gym into the open air and onto a small boat deck. The 'micro compact home' is informed by the traditional needs of a home and transportation design. We find that 'pairing' is a strong factor in guiding innovation. There is another aspect of 'between-ness' that we cultivate at TU Munich. Eero Saarinen said that 'Architecture consists largely of the art of placing an object between earth and sky', and one thinks immediately of his masterpieces, Dulles Airport and the St. Louis Arch. We ask our students to see and assess their own work and to value it in this way. Though many architectural students are trained to use a computer today, we train our students to view their work as an outsider and beyond the computer screen, to be their own critics and to really use their eyes to learn.

AV

prof. richard horden

micro architecture | 35

RUTAN VARIEZE

'Visibility' is an important word in our programme, as we encourage students to take very seriously the powers of visual quality and observation.

'Beauty' Visual observation necessarily leads to issues of beauty. At the Institute, and in general, the word has two meanings: beauty in aesthetics and beauty in function. It requires courage to use the word and to be able to discuss whether or not something has or does not have beauty, but without the debate there is no chance of achieving something exceptional. We use the word frequently, always aware of the dual meaning. A Rutan VariEze is beautiful to look at and is also extraordinarily beautiful and graceful to fly. With its single stick and no rudder pedals, it is also very simple to fly, as the name ('very easy') implies. This is the objective of micro architecture, to grant the skill to the student to create something that is beautiful to an untrained eye and also simple and beautiful in its use. People must smile when they see a project. Beauty is infinite and independent of time and material. A study of it would be like the study of the universe or of the micro universe: indefinable because of infinite change. Our opportunities to create beauty change with every moment, as new materials and new aesthetics unfold with time. I often notice the beauty of an airport runway at night with blue and green point lights recessed in the dimmed apron surface and see the gracefully moving white-winged objects playing a slow, highly controlled ballet. This is very much a vision of the modern age. We have this beauty, and though masters of the past, such as Leonardo and Michelangelo created works of incomparable beauty, they never beheld such a site as this. I wonder how it might have motivated them. Even with due reverence for the past, we must discover and create the beauties of our own age.

opposite page:
airport by night;
wing of an aircraft

Aviation As a designer I have long felt an affinity to the aviation industry, where I have often found almost ideal combinations of beauty in form and function. Since the delightful flights in the Jet Ranger 'Whisky Mike' with Norman Foster in the 1980s and in the Aerospatiale Lama with the Swiss Alpine helicopter pilots delivering our 'Ski Haus' project to the high mountains in the early 1990s, my interest in the industry has only grown. Aviation is in-built with a need for precision and this precision is not only to do with the essential technical aspects but is carried through the industry to influence everything from graphic design, to crew presentation, cutlery design, communication, airport design and, in the best airlines, elegant new ideas in food preparation and presentation. I feel strongly that we can learn from techniques in minimizing waste in material, food and fuel. Because of its precision, we sometimes call the 'micro compact home' 'an instrument for living'.

RH

RH

prof. richard horden **introduction**

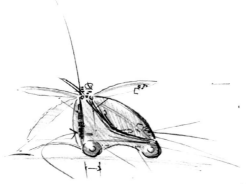

Like a Swiss watch, the compact function and beauty are integral to the product. I am fortunate to experience driving in the Swissair Smart™ car and taking regular weekly flights with high-quality airlines like Swiss Airlines and Lufthansa over the Alps between Zurich and Munich. These things help nurture my strong appreciation for the design quality that accompanies the best aviation experiences in which a well-designed cabin and accessories fit perfectly with the taut and elegant design of the airport as in, for example, Munich Franz J. Strauss and Zürich Kloten.

The director of Munich Franz Josef Strauss, voted best airport in Europe for the past three years, Andreas Sander-Carqueville, explains their philosophy as 'seamless travel'. Thanks to Andreas Sander-Carqueville and his team, for the past 11 years we have been able to take our students on a tour of the entire airport, not only to inspect the impressive buildings up close, but to see how the many elements of such a tremendous infrastructure are made to work for individual passengers. It was in 2000, while we made the July tour as usual inside the giant glass, 200-metre-span maintenance hangar, that we came across the crew rest cabin for the long-haul Airbus A340. This is basically a toughened airfreight container that has been modified by Eurocopter to accommodate four crew beds for long-haul flights. Built of aluminium with excellent task lighting, flat-screen information panels and a sound system to link the rest crew to the main deck, the cabin measures only 1.5m in height, similar to the seat areas at the window position in most aircraft. I was fascinated by the chance to make a living 'cabin' with the same principles. Eurocopter were contacted by our team and information was gathered which eventually led to the design of the 'micro compact home' and other micro architecture projects.

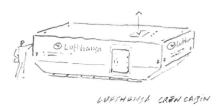

LUFTHANSA CREW CABIN

Transportation and architecture Buildings for transport and habitation have always been closely related. As far back as the early Saxons, church structures were informed by the up-turned hulls of longboats. More recently, Le Corbusier developed ideas from ships, automobiles and early aircraft designs. Norman Foster describes parallels with architecture and aviation in the organization of architecture. And one of the most widely published new buildings in Europe, the BMW World building, by Coop Himmelb(l)au, follows the current edged sculptured forms of recent model BMW cars. These are not exceptions, and it is only natural that when looking to design buildings efficiently, we continue to build on the advances made in engineering and aerodynamics in the transportation industry.

Micro architecture allows us to tap into this area of innovation, and benefits not only from research in form and materials but in the development of prefabrication methods. The micro compact home and, in future, the family compact home, can be built in a factory where the construction and use of materials is much more controlled and efficient. The factory method also offers the opportunity to fit furniture to architecture in a more integrated and functional use of space. This is not a new concept. The Romans did not use chairs, but rather built inclined couches made of stone, which were covered with textile and served as a fixed place for meals and meetings. These might contain a carved place for the wine goblet and food. The table was also of stone and located within arm's reach from the couch. The 'micro compact home' has integrated table, bed and seating and, as with a car, boat or aircraft, there is no need to buy furniture. This holistic approach is a fundamental part of micro architecture teaching. In addition to designing a small building, students develop skills in integrated product design.

The Future of Micro The pressure to reduce carbon emissions will mean our consideration for minimum mass becomes a factor in building and engineering processes, and not only in the aerospace industries. The building process must become more efficient. Though most buildings use some prefabricated components they are specific to their site and so are essentially one-off prototypes. One of the advantages of a course in micro architecture is that in developing a micro architecture prototype students may be producing a component or module that can be used in further building and design, and help us towards the goal of building more efficiently. They also come away with a clear understanding of the whole process and sequence of building as well as the decision-making and time pressures involved in seeing a project through to completion.

Another benefit of micro architecture studies is that it offers the opportunity for students to take part in design and factory supervision. Factory-produced components for large-scale buildings include modules such as glass-and-aluminium cladding panels for office buildings, long balconies for residential buildings or toilet/bathroom pods for hotels and hospitals. Our graduates who have experience of overseeing the fabrication of prototypes are of great value to an architectural or design office involved in this type of building.

There are many careers that an architectural student can enter today, including product design, robotics, logistics and project management. Micro architecture broadens the student experience from model-making and CAD drawing to compact product manufacture, and exposes them to the all-important transition from 2D design to 3D construction together with experienced partners from industry.

Micro architecture is a rich learning environment for students and for teachers. It may also prove to be useful ground for further studies in industrial production where the young architect is able to research robotics and enhance the process of factory production of buildings. Our first doctoral candidate at the Institute will be Nadine Zinser and the title of her thesis is 'Micro Architecture and Transportation Design'.

TU Munich is one of the three elite universities in Germany and with its very high skills in production processes and design and beautiful geographic location similar to ETH Zurich it has one of the best situations in central Europe for the founding of a new graduate 'European design school for the future generations'.

RH, Zürichsee, June 2008

prof. richard horden **introduction**

micro architecture | studio

micro
architecture
teaching

The Studio Generally we have around 45 students in the studio, 250 for lectures, and a healthy mix of pre-degree and novice students. They are seen every week by our five teaching assistants, who are themselves fully qualified architects, and myself every Tuesday and Wednesday.

Language English is the language most used at the Institute, and is certainly required at presentations. We have a lecturer in English-language courses, Rosemarie Fitzgibbon, and her studio is open to German and foreign students. Most German students speak very acceptable English, and the University president, Wolfgang A. Herrmann, supports lectures and teaching in English for practical reasons: to encourage students to find work abroad following their studies. Many of these work in our London office during vacations and after studies, and with Foster and Partners and other UK, Australian and US practices.

Prof. R. Horden,
Heinz Richter,
Dyfed Griffiths,
Nadine Zinser and
Burkhard Franke
at *schlusskritik*

I enjoy exploring the origins and comparisons between German and English, and we often use a mix of the two languages to give a special quality to a name and communicate something of its geographic origins, such as, for example, for the 'Ski Haus' (see page 116). In German the correct term would be *Schi Haus*; in English it would be 'Ski House'. Another example is 'Reed Huis' ('Reed House') (see page 246), a mix of English and Dutch, for a project that was inspired by and designed for the Netherlands. We generally use two short words for titles as this is most precise, attractive and memorable.

Briefing We begin every semester, two semesters in one calendar year (winter: mid-October to February; and summer: mid-April to July), with a careful briefing session that is accompanied by the handout of a paper and digital instruction brochure. This is an A4 page folded twice into an airline format 21 x 10cm, informed by the Swissair timetable. The brochure is prepared by one of the assistants responsible for the project with guidance from myself. The briefing and brochure outline the project specification and location geography and key references and bibliography. This also sometimes contains sketches and starter guide diagrams for the students. The micro compact home brochure, in 2001 called 'Tokyo 26', contained very specific sketches and diagrams and the precise dimension of 2.6m for the cube home.

Presentations We ask students to present their work on A3-size paper or digitally, to reduce paper wastage, and to produce their own 'marketing brochure' a similar 21 x 10cm format at the final presentation. This involves the students in graphic design from the beginning, an essential element to the presentation of architecture at any level. Full formal presentations are made every two weeks with informal table critiques between. Guest lecturers are invited to inform and critique the students and attend the key mid-term presentation and final critiques, *Schlusstestat*.

System 26 At the start of our teaching in November 1996 I designed a table and screen system, now referred to as 'System 26' (see page 296). This consists of light and low A0 x A1 size aluminium-framed tables on castors on a light grey carpet. The mobility of these tables is an important ingredient in the teaching. Students work in groups of 1–4 and are trained to arrange their tables precisely to optimize their presentation needs. Large models, for example, are kept to one side and rolled into position when required, so the student architect is also the architect of his or her own space. The low noise level in the studio helps for a calm atmosphere. Low tables help visual clarity and informality. Small tables encourage intimacy in discussion and debates between students, assistants and professor. The tables' precision and lightness communicate the qualities we value in design. The table is the first micro architecture that the students encounter. 'System 26' is now used for exhibitions and degree presentations and has been used in our London office since 1985.

this page:
'System 26' and
exhibition at TUM

opposite page:
breakfast at the studio

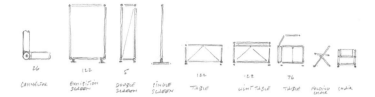

Studio breakfast A regular event at the start of the semester is the studio breakfast. The 'System 26' tables are arranged into a long 'feast shape'. This is a time for personal introductions between students, assistants and professor and we all exchange our first thoughts about the design topic and show inspiration images, research and build very rough concept models. It is also a good time for the professor to guide the project and define the way forward. There may be three or four quite different topics, with totally variant geographies for design in the semester and it requires focus and mental agility to be concise and precise in giving positive helpful direction to the students. The breakfast is also an opportunity to introduce the facilities in our technical centre. Tim Wessbecher, an architect/assistant and highly skilled model builder, briefs the students in the use of the CNC machines etc.

UF

75m 35 KNOT ECO. MARTIN FRANCIS

Student mix In every semester there is a healthy mix of foreign and local Munich students, no more so than last semester when we had 14 nationalities in a total group of only 40 students! We have regular, English-speaking student exchanges between Bath University in England, University of Champagne Illinois, the University of Wellington, New Zealand, and now the Arts Institute at Bournemouth, England. Israeli students are frequent visitors and South American, Japanese and Chinese students now more so.

Collaboration with clients and foreign universities Many projects are the product of an invitation to collaborate with German and European industries and organizations or with foreign universities. 'Peak Lab' (see page 132) was a result of an invitation from Professor Ulrich Pfammatter at the HTA Lucerne, to join with his students in the design for a high-altitude research lab near Zermatt. The astronaut workstation was a collaboration between Professor Igenbergs, the Director of the Aerospace Institute at the TU Munich, with Hans Huber, and from Constance Adams at Lockheed Martin and David Ray at NASA's Johnson Space Center. The Antarctica projects came about from an invitation from the Alfred Wegener Institute in Bremerhaven to develop alternative fast-construction methods for building at the two German Antarctic stations. The 'micro compact home' (see page 232) was realized after an invitation from Dieter Massberg from the Student Housing Authority in Munich. The 'ice camp' in Greenland from Lotte Bjerregaad at the DTU, Denmark; the New Zealand beach project from Roy Fleetwood, a former colleague from my time at Norman Foster's office, who is now based at the University of Wellington.

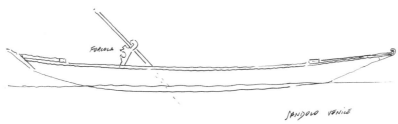

FORCOLA

SANDOLO VENICE

Visiting lecturers Our guest lecturers are not only selected from the architectural profession. The carbon-fibre boat projects were guided by Gilberto Penzo from Venice, a historian of Venetian boats and author of the book *The Gondola*, and by Martin Francis, the designer of the world's fastest private yacht, *Eco*. Others have included Marcus Spinnler, a solar energy consultant, Mathias Junghanns from BMW Design Works, Dirk Schmauzer, a former designer for Porsche Design, and many others.

Coaching vs. Teaching During the period of establishing micro architecture in 1996/97 we often discussed the issue of how intensely to guide the students. To an English person that would seem surprising; however, in Germany it is quite common for professors to abandon the students with little help or guidance, leaving them to fend for themselves and inform them only at the intermediate and final testats. We hold table crits and full presentations on a weekly basis and often intervene to indicate to the student how it is possible and necessary to make quantum changes during the design process. For example, during the development of the boat project, one group was floundering with a problematic hull shape. Nadine Zinser, one of the team of assistants who had done some exquisite research into this topic, guided one of the groups towards possible drive systems and hull shapes introducing them to the classic Americas' Cup and 'Wally' vertical bow, sloped and cantilever stern. This helped the students to gain confidence in their project and resulted in an outstanding presentation by the students at the Düsseldorf boat show in 2006 and completion of their boat in 2008.

The question of how much guidance is constructive is much debated in the team, and quite often I am criticized by the assistants for over-guidance. However, my philosophy is not to hold back. I feel that in being open and honest with the students you gain a deep respect for one another. For that reason, I don't waste time with politesse. My experience of working with Norman Foster, the best teacher I ever had, helped shaped this view. He would often

studio

prof. richard horden

'zu tisch'

say, 'you would not like it if we built it that way', or he would communicate precise design and details by executing a rapid and elegant pencil sketch in front of the individual or team. There is, I feel, a decision that has to be made between achieving a high degree of quality for the student group or allowing the students to 'park' themselves into mediocrity. Of course, much depends upon the students' ability to listen and act on advice or not. My belief is to give the students and assistants the full benefit of my own experience, knowledge and skill. We find that the high-quality students are careful listeners and are the ones who move their projects on to a new stage with speed and precision without dwelling on previous, unworkable ideas. There are also those elite students who surprise us with their ability to move the project on to a more advanced stage every week, who are always looking forward to new ways to improve their designs. For them life only has 'fast forward'; there is no reverse gear!

Presentations and table crits *zu tisch* In the micro architecture programme, studio professor and assistants see the students' work every week during the semester. Visual and verbal presentation techniques are a vital part of architectural life in an office and we ask our students to prepare for this by making formal presentations to the whole studio every two weeks. The intervening week is used for group table crits. This schedule enables all the students in the studio to see their own project within the context of others and as the students are well-mixed ninth-semester, pre-diploma students with fifth-semester students in the same studio – the younger students can benefit from the knowledge and experience of the students from upper school. We provide the students with pin panels and white space above for digital projection and the mobile 'System 26' tables on castors for models. Architectural design, graphic design, form and colour control are all discussed and assessed during these presentations for the benefit of the whole group of up to 60 students.

'm-ch' patent for the USA

Patents There is a legal framework for all students and professors at the TU Munich but in the first instance essentially all designs belong to the University. The University will finance a patent if they feel the product is worthy of that, and give the student or professor the right to 30 or 40 per cent of any benefit that may accrue. This is subject to an evaluation period, after the design is complete, of three to four months when the University decides whether or not to adopt and finance the design or hand it back to the professor or student to fund their own patent with full rights. If a professor instructs his or her students and assistants to undertake a design or research leading to an invention, he or she becomes the 'the author'. If a student undertakes a design without being instructed in the first instance by his professor then that student becomes 'the author'. In any event, the professor or student has to apply to the University Patent Department to evaluate and assist in the way forward. The University is geared mainly to chemical, mechanical, electrical or physics-based patents. Architectural patents are few and far between and much less remunerative for the University. The student or professor has at some stage to face the reality of the cost and complications of a patent. For example the 'micro compact home' patent and trademarks cost in the region of 35,000 euro and requires renewal every year of around 3,000 euro.

The 'micro compact home' patent followed this same process. As I had initiated, with precise sketches in the briefing brochure, and supervised the design, the University granted me the sole right to patent. The 'TU_FiN' (see page 174) boat project patent, however, was granted to the students, and the astronaut workstation was not patented as the seat restraint was already owned and patented by Professor Igenbergs at the Institute for Aerospace at the TU Munich. We did, however, insist on the signing of a non-declaration agreement with NASA Johnson Space Center.

studio

prof. richard horden

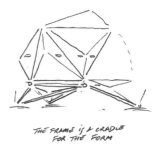

THE FRAME IS A CRADLE
FOR THE FORM

Research/new product design In a large architectural school like the TU Munich with 1,000 students and 30 professors there are fundamentally two types of research. The first is industrial research funded, for example, by corporations with an interest in product design, such as BMW or Siemens. The second type is PhD research, which is carried out by a single postgraduate student working directly with a professor for two or three years. However, I strive to promote a third type of research, which I refer to as 'academic research', and which happens in the delightfully intimate environment in which the students work directly with a professor and assistants to create a new architectural product. The micro compact home is now perhaps the most widely known example of this type of research carried out by our programme.

Natural setting and 'three-point support' Students select their own sites and have to analyse the natural environment before starting form studies, internal planning and technical development. They are required to photograph and accumulate sunlight path diagrams, topographic, historical and foundation strata. We require the students to separate their micro architecture from the landscape even when the ground they are building on is almost vertical. In most circumstances we ask the students to use adjustable, three-point supports. There are several benefits to this: stability, with fast adjustment and installation, visual transparency and minimal interruption with the natural landscape. In addition, access from below is sheltered, an especially important feature for Antarctica and extreme situations. Three-point support also leads to the concept of triangulation and therefore a better understanding of this essential fact of stability in structures and the most efficient and therefore lightest weight and materially reduced form.

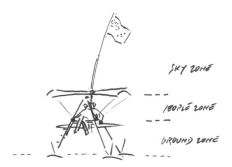

When raised above the ground the project is perceived more as an object so that architecture then becomes product design. The end result must have clarity in form and must complement nature visually, as well as in energy usage and carbon emissions. These requirements force a discussion about form. It takes time to appreciate the importance of this basic fact of architecture and structure, but the approach helps to provide students with a feel for structure and stability especially when constructing material models.

'Zoning' The three vertical zones of a building are the ground zone, the peopled zone and the sky zone. These essentially different parts must function in their own right and be visually expressed and coordinated to produce a harmonious composition. There are the other three technical zonings, more complex to describe briefly as they must exist in three dimensions, for movement, circulation and flow, structure zones and services zones. Clarity in plan zoning, for example, saying 'the kitchen should be close to the entrance of a small home', is good advice. In zoning of functions, the four spaces for sleep, hygiene, food preparation and work, are carefully grouped in the sequence of use and overlap in a harmonious and intriguing way in the micro compact home. Micro architecture is also the study of the efficient zoning of compact and complex spaces similar to the disciplines in the car industry and aircraft industries.

studio

prof. richard horden

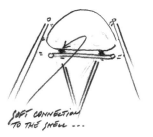

Soft connection to the shell ...

Phrase bytes In order to communicate efficiently in the time-pressured environment in-studio when there are often only a few minutes to catch up with a design, we use shorthand and oft-repeated phrases. Following the format for the titles of the micro architecture projects these are usually made up of a few words that clearly summarize a complex concept. For example, the first dimension of architecture is light, the natural sunlight that gives highlight and shade, warmth (1.5 kilos of sunlight are enough to power the whole earth for one day), orientation and visual beauty to any project.

We use the terms **'licht and leicht'**. Light has two meanings in English: 'luminosity' and 'lightness of weight'. In German, these meanings are expressed as *licht und leicht*, in Italian, *luce e leggero*. Micro architecture training is about using light in both senses: optimizing natural light and minimizing material use. We also use the phrase **'touch the earth lightly'** as a guiding principle. And in my introduction I have referred to the German word *zwischen* which we use to describe projects that exist between different technologies.

'If it looks good it is good' Although there are intrinsic dangers in the use of this phrase, we still use it in the studio. It is derived from the aeronautical industry where engineers are trained, or have the natural skill, to develop an intuition to spot when there is something right or wrong in a design. There is value again in that it makes the architectural student look twice at what he or she may think is perfect and a reminder that if it looks good means that it must also function well. Generally I use the phrase to drive the students in this way: 'If it looks good you have a chance to get sponsorship, if it doesn't you don't.'

'aesthetics and an-aesthetics' The word 'an-aesthetics' is defined in the dictionary as 'without perception', so aesthetics must be 'with perception'. It is as simple as that! We train our students in the art of developed perception, to work to inform, to learn. Architects and students of architecture have to learn to 'read buildings' by looking at them, and as we develop an eye for reading architecture, we develop the same for reading other things, products, cars, yachts and nature, most especially nature.

Form studies We know that the human eye appreciates the primary forms, particles of primary forms, symmetry, proportion and balance in an asymmetrical composition. At the Institute we often begin studies with analysis in relation to the six Platonic solids. This enables a student to define the limits of their project, and, for some, the constraint of working with a pure form helps them to move forward. It can mean the discovery of how to place elements within a primary form.

A micro home project was designed by a group starting from a tetrahedron, and the students made the discovery that there can be no vertical partitions; these must follow the geometry of the primary solid. Such a discovery makes the project move forward at a faster pace to a delightful conclusion with details and full-size mock-ups.

studio

prof. richard horden

Human perception Our eyes are arranged horizontally, not vertically, in order to give a wide horizontal field of view. This protects us from sudden attack or from predators, like automobiles! It means that we see more width than height. We tend towards an affinity for the horizontal which becomes extremely important in micro architecture where dimensions are tight, and horizontals give width to a small space. The micro compact home interior is about the alignment of the horizontal edges and surfaces of shelves, bed and table. Natural and artificial light in the 'm-ch' (see page 232) is always directed at the horizontal plane. This generates window positions and dimensions, as too much daylight is as destructive as too little. We avoid the use of top light in small spaces as this creates heavy shadows under the eyes, nose and chin, and makes us feel 'radiated' from above rather than 'informed' from the side. Top light can make even large spaces feel small.

this page:
Aerospatiale Lama
helicopter; Swissair
Smart™ car, RH

opposite page:
Munich Airport, T2;
Swiss Airbus A330

RH

RH

Aviation design and architecture I wrote in the introduction about how much we can learn from the successful designs in the aviation industry where precision is a necessary achievement. Precision is at the heart of the design of the micro compact home: in human scale and product design, in colour, LED lighting, minimal energy use and detailing and in precisely zoning the four principal human functions: sleep, hygiene, food preparation and work. The images here illustrate the way transport and architecture are closely related to one another at any point in history. We teach observation of transportation design, and now transport designers watch us! The 'Ski Haus' (see page 116) design borrows ideas from the Swiss Aerospatiale Lama helicopter, and the Airbus A330, as well as the Alpine chalet and Zermatt grain store. This just goes to show that good design does not exist alone; it is developed out of a precise examination of its natural and manmade surroundings.

RH

SWISS

studio

prof. richard horden

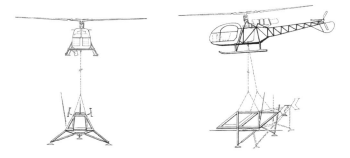

Delivery method In micro architecture, one of the first issues that comes up in the design process is the delivery method. The 'Ski Haus' (see page 116), for example, is delivered and removed by helicopter. So micro architecture projects have to start with dimensional and weight constraints that come from standard modes of transport. The 'micro compact home' and event centre are delivered by truck (so have to be around 2.6m wide), the 'M-igloo' (see page 204) by Ski-Doo, the 'iPod House' (see page 168) and 'New Zealand Out-Bach' (a weekend home; see page 198) by ISO container, so they have the constraints of 2.3w x 2.5h and 8–12m long. Weight and dimensions are valuable and highly specific constraints on the design process, and these primary considerations lead to a greater understanding of reducing mass of material and strength and efficiency in structure.

this page:
helicopter
approaching the
'Ski Haus'

opposite page:
elevation of apartments
on the River Thames

RH

RH

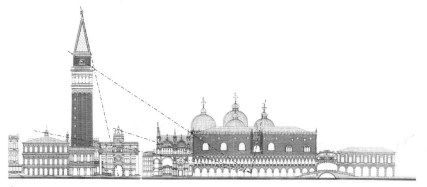

Cross-referencing In a taught urban environment it is uplifting to relate a new design to adjacent buildings (as well as considering natural forms), in scale, in proportion or in tones, colours or materials. The diagram illustrates how the buildings that surround the Doge's Palace are arranged to complement the most important building in Venice with implied diagonals, using the same compositional principles as in Renaissance painting. One of the projects currently being executed by my London firm, Horden Cherry Lee, for the River Thames in London uses this principle in the asymmetric composition of the new building next to the well-known Somerset House, a classical listed building. We also used this referencing principle in 1990 when designing the Queen's Stand which related quite deliberately in scale to the modular balconies of the Edwardian Prince's Stand located adjacent and to the west.

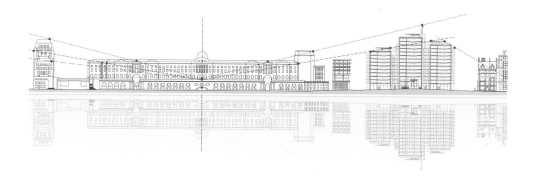

© COOP HIMMELB(L)AU

generation of form

In striving for both innovation and beauty, it is one of the overall goals of our Institute to explore a modern architectural language that gives adequate expression to the fast-developing world around us. The word 'form' plays a central role in teaching at the Institute although this little word seems to have been abandoned from larger parts of the theoretical architectural discussion.

In our opinion, the well-established rectangular box cannot be the only architectural solution in a society where a product such as the automobile so beautifully reflects the aesthetic and technological possibilities of our time, and while the seemingly unlimited power of the computer allows for the creation of the architect's wildest dreams! One example of this type of imaginative form, the recent BMW Welt building by Coop Himmelb(l)au has brought a kind of architecture to Munich that would have been out of reach only 20 years ago. Of course our students are influenced by this kind of architectural fireworks and they use the possibility of

this page:
BMW Welt, Munich,
Coop Himmelb(l)au,
2007

opposite page:
Richard Horden
sketching primary
forms during a work-
shop in Silvaplana in
2006; a balloon form
study of an upside
down pyramid

BF

being at our institute to jump courageously into the world of free forms. Though this does not mean that they are immediately successful in employing their newfound shapes: the first crits of a new semester often turn out to be disappointing, as even if students have managed to deliver a beautiful foam model, they may not be able to reproduce the form or to simply describe how they generated it. At this point, instead of returning to the box, we guide the students to simplify their project and to concentrate on classic rules of geometry. That might sound old fashioned, but the most important thing in teaching is to give the students the control over what they are doing. So while we encourage experimentation with form, it is experimentation with understanding. The computer can generate any spatial object you ask it to, but the architect needs to develop a rational or intuitive understanding of the form to make it buildable. Simple or complex, engineer or sculptor: beauty has to do with control!

BF

BF

dipl. ing. burkhard franke

The Sydney Opera House is a well-known example of the use of geometry to produce an exciting building shape. Jörn Utzon's prize-winning design of shapes that replicate billowing sails was made into a piece of buildable architecture when he transformed the free shells of the original design into sections of a sphere – a truly simple form only described by one length, the radius. The design was created in the early 1960s, long before the computer widely extended the architectural possibilities, but the strategy of using simple geometries to create a complex and rich architectural form is still applicable today.

Simplification is not necessary, of course, if you begin with a simple form. Probably 95 per cent of all buildings are based on a rectangular spatial grid, so-called 'boxes'. We are used to working inside the Cartesian grid – measuring by length, width and height – and tend to extrude vertical walls from a rectangular plan. So it is a big step from there to developing architecture

BF

JU

from a simple Platonic solid, though these are seemingly the simplest geometric objects imaginable. A form based on triangles, however, is spatially much more difficult to handle and in fact also more difficult to use. On the other hand forms like a tetrahedron or an octahedron offer a much higher static performance compared with a cube.

At the Institute we have developed different projects from Platonic solid shapes: the 'One Kilo House' (see page 188) and the 'Skypod' are pyramids (half tetrahedrons); the 'Polar Lab' (see page 206) and the 'Octa' are based on an octahedron. They all turned out to be spatially very challenging but achieved a beauty based on a balance between simplicity and complexity.

Many of our students do not start their project with a simple geometric form. In fact, we encourage them to develop their design from an object or living thing that demonstrates beauty and a link to the topic of the design. These sources tend to be formally very complex. Typical

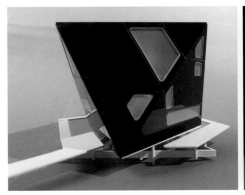 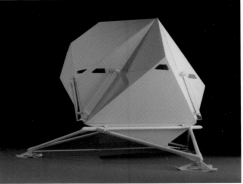

examples from nature are birds, mussels, or trees; while technical sources might be sailboats, birds or aircraft. These forms cannot be simplified to an easily managed geometric object in one step, but the team of students, assistants and professor find a way to identify the inherent character of the form, whether it lies in its effect or simply its purpose.

For the project on this page, which was called 'Wrap House', the students chose a pasta form as an image for the little weekend house they had to design, an object, which is already derivative of a mussel. It didn't seem appropriate to just adapt the form, so we found a new shape which maintained the object's key properties, such as giving shelter, offering closed and open spaces, and doing this with a three-dimensionally shaped surface. In order to gain control over the design process, we defined a triangular surface that was folded six times, with the folds not parallel to each other. The sharp corners were softened by applying different radii. Finally

this page:
the initial image, paper folding studies and the final model of the 'Wrap House' (Julia Wolf and Daniel Haimerl)

opposite page:
form-finding sketches by Richard Horden and Burkhard Franke;
two working models of the 'Silvaglider' project

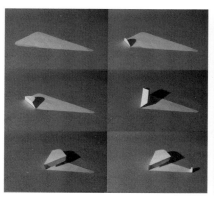

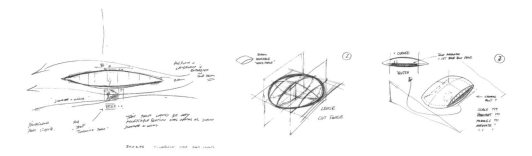

a form was achieved that offered an enclosed living space with an adjacent terrace. Since this form wouldn't want to sit on the ground, it was supported by a central mast, connecting both ends of the continuous surface.

The sketches above demonstrate how the idea for a form is generated and controlled in the designer's head, not in a computer. In the 'Silvaglider' project, the basic idea of the eye-like elevation was there from the beginning. The sketches show the form-finding process from an object with two single curved surfaces to a more sophisticated shell that is curved in two directions. This 'pill' shape was then cut on either side to make façade openings. To finally check the form, the two variations were digitally modelled in 3D, the volumes were CNC-milled and finally vacuum formed. We decided to go for the double curved surfaces which were, in this early design stage, simple sphere segments, just like the Sydney Opera House.

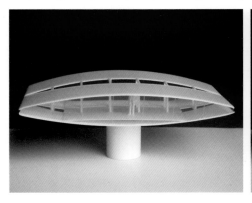

learning from nature

Looking at the Institute's projects of the past 12 years it is easy to see that the majority of them were not designed for urban situations but for a natural context. That is not only because an architectural artifact looks more beautiful in a natural landscape. Richard Horden constantly reminds the students (and the assistants) that nature is an inexhaustible reservoir for inspiration. There are two main aspects of forms in nature we can learn from: that it creates beautiful forms and that these are intelligent solutions to meeting the demands of its surroundings. These qualities are two sides of the same coin, and are expressed also in a maxim often uttered by Prof. Richard Horden during our crits: 'If it looks good, it is good'.

The aspect of aesthetics in nature is quite obvious: we associate nature in a positive way with an environment that feels untouched by man and nobody would question the aesthetics of a maple seed, a bird or a smoothly water-worn pebble. The latter, in fact, gave the inspiration

this page:
a water-sanded pebble (above), a maple seed and an albatross – natural aerodynamic objects associated with beauty

opposite page:
the 'Solar Pebble' project (above);
the Olympic roof in Munich, Frei Otto, 1972

RH

for the 'Solar Pebble' project (see page 260), which gains its form from the smooth but irregular rounded stone. However, the beauty of nature is not as simplistic as it might sound nor can it be referred to as an isolated phenomena. It is embedded in a system of extremely complex rules of which we have only understood relatively few, despite centuries of human research. The German architect Frei Otto, who designed the giant acrylic canopies for the Olympic Games in Munich in 1972, has a remarkably scientific way of working. He spent his life trying to translate natural solutions into architecture. Similar to the scientific discipline of bionics, he started to analyse the coherent effects of natural systems and applied them by technological means.

These achievements influence our work at the Institute, but looking back at more than six years of teaching with Prof. Horden, I realize we like to follow another approach to learn from nature, a more playful one.

BF

studio

dipl. ing. burkhard franke

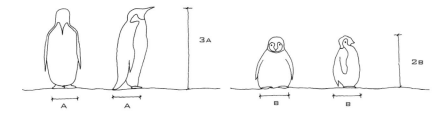

At the beginning of a new semester we have our students begin their new project with a week of research. They often decide to use a natural form for inspiration, so they have to get an overview of the chosen natural phenomena relating to their project. Though time is usually short and we want to make the step into architecture as soon as possible, this is an important first step, and we regard this research phase as a tool to develop ideas for a design concept. However, it is not meant to live up to scientific standards! We look at a natural form long enough to make plausible assumptions about things, such as where it comes from and how it functions, etc. While a scientist would have to prove that a particular belief is true, for us the assumption is valid as an 'idea generator' even if it might be close to naivety. I remember Richard Horden saying that he tries to preserve the naivety of children in his thinking, which means a way of looking at the world with new understanding.

this page:
adult and baby
penguins (above);
'water form' and 'land
form'; the 'Ice Station'
project

opposite page:
the 'Silva Spider'
project (above); the
'Cocoon' project with
reference image (see
page 200)

Doug Allan | The Image Bank | Getty Images   Konrad Wothe | Minden Pictures | Getty Images

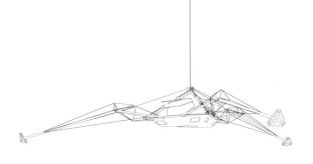

The form-finding process for the polar station is a good example of this straightforward handling of scientific knowledge. While researching the environment, the students found a reference to the streamlined adult penguin as a 'water form' because its body shape moves so well in water. The shorter and thicker penguin chick, who cannot yet swim, however, was described as a 'land form', and therefore a perfect shape for an arctic station.

Further study found that because the baby penguin does not move very much, it needs a compact form that helps retain body heat, another important feature when designing for areas of extreme cold. In the final design of the 'Ice Station' project (see page 210), the relationship to the form of the penguin chick is still visible. In the same way, the 'Silva Spider' project (see page 122) was informed by the basic shape and movements of a spider, though it may not look and move exactly like a spider. Both projects still clearly show a close formal link to their natural origin.

studio

dipl. ing. burkhard franke

BF

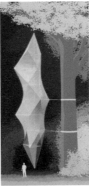

However, the 'Desert Lodge' (see page 224), a design for the Namibian Desert is an example of a more abstract relation. Its technological appearance was inspired by the shape of a lizard, who lifts his forefeet to minimize contact with the hot ground and turns his protected back into the sun, thus shading his sensitive underbelly. From this general idea, we developed a scheme of an inclined building with a wide solar collector directed into the sun, absorbing energy and protecting the rooms, which are glazed on the shady side. The final result is a technological object for the desert, which exhibits a high degree of recognition and efficiency. The 'Desert Lodge' is a successful example of learning from a natural form, not by copying it but by reading it and translating it from a natural image into an architectural one.

A different approach is demonstrated in the project called 'Drift' which came out of an attempt to start a project from an object that had been found on site, an 'object trouvé'. The object here was a wooden root, nothing spectacular in terms of form, and with no conceptual connection to the task of a weekend house. The aim of the project was to demonstrate how to develop an inhabitable object from a random shape and learn how to control the form. Since no geometrical rules could be applied, the students started the design process with a detailed scan of the object and subsequently transformed it in two parallel work streams. On one hand they approached it in an analogous manner, building models while constantly controlling the aesthetics and usability of the form. On the other hand, they digitally reduced the number of triangles of the spatial mesh, milling the form on the CNC machine, and checking again the form using a bidirectional design process that included digital reduction and sculptural ambition.

By this seemingly whimsical exercise, the students were able to learn ways to approach almost any form, to develop strategies to understand it and finally to control it for the purpose at hand.

this page:
Namibian lizard
and section of the
'Desert Lodge'

opposite page:
the 'object trouvé' and
the form transformation
process with analog
and digital models
for the 'Drift' project
(Annalena Priester, Lisa
Thaler, Benjamin Rantz)

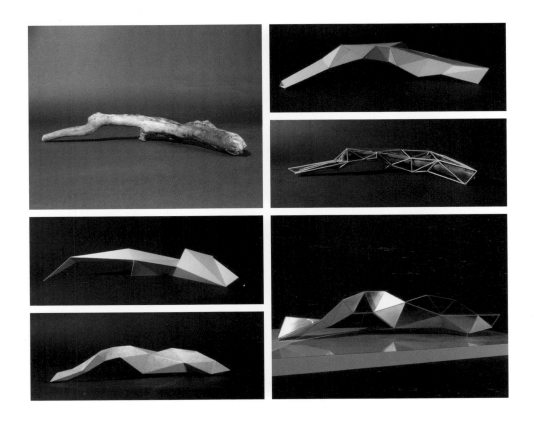

Courtesy of Apple

architecture and product design

The separation between the disciplines of architecture and product design can be considered as a matter of scale. From the point of view of designing an object, is there a real difference between a caravan and a house, a chair and a bridge or between a bowl and a stadium? The way we use things and the cultural understanding of our environment tell us when we should talk about architecture or product design, but effectively there is no such distinction necessary. In Richard Horden's programme we therefore like to speak of micro architecture as 'product design for the environment'. This term is very useful also because it indicates a link between a piece of architecture and its environment, and furthermore it makes clear that one has an impact on the other.

When it comes to arranging functions inside an imaginary space, forming units of components that belong together while others are grouped and located in a different manner, depend-

this page:
Apple mouse (above);
Allianz Arena, Munich

opposite page:
production facility;
welding robot

Allianz Arena | B. Ducke

ing on their role inside a complex technical organism, and giving the whole a unique envelope that reflects the particular sense of the object, where is the difference between designing an architectural object or a product?

Of course there are some aspects still to be discussed. Do we talk about a singular object or about the production of a series of thousands of pieces? The means of producing a piece of architecture have improved tremendously during the last decades. Yet, even though robotics have found their way into building construction as well as prefabrication of components, and the production of whole building units has become a relatively standard building technique, we are still far away from being able to produce architecture with the precision, speed and quality of mass production as we know it from car factories or similar industrial plants.

HM   HM

architecture and product design | 73

The beauty of an object is often determined by the degree of precision that it has achieved for its purpose. There is an endless variety of examples in nature from which we can try to learn about the production of beautiful objects to enhance our lives. Form as a dimension in architecture and product design plays a key role in our understanding of a (complex) object. The first impression, association and emotion created by the visual shape, surface and colour can never be revised and greatly influences our overall attitude to a building or product. But beyond the surface or exterior form, there is an inside to every form we create, and with architecture the inside quite often becomes more important than the outside. The people living in a house or an apartment will be more interested in their interior living environment than in the way it might look from the outside. Nevertheless, there is a strong relationship between both worlds, and the impression that comes from the external shape and visual impression should be reflected

this page:
BMW convertible
(above); predetermined
shape; life happens
inside ...

opposite page:
small private jet;
aeroplane interior

Loungepark | Stone | Getty Images

in the interior. The interior dimension has many interacting aspects to be considered carefully – the condition of natural and artificial light throughout the day and year, the sound, touch and feel of material, colour and surface, the condition and temperature of the climate, to name only the most important ones. If we look at product interiors as compared with architecture, for instance in a modern car or aircraft, it becomes evident that there is a lot more to achieve in architecture than we are able to perform today. To get closer to those high-quality, precision interiors, we might consider the concept of a coat that surrounds us day to day. The very basic understanding of architecture as nothing more than an additional layer of protection from the outside (besides our skin and clothes) gives some idea of the importance of the issue, trying to make that immediate environment comfortable and enjoyable at the same time should be motivation enough to keep moving forward!

dipl. ing. hendrik müller

© Eclipse Aviation Corporation, 2008

© Eclipse Aviation Corporation, 2008

habitation and transportation

Our Institute is placed between the fields of architecture and product design. We are researching and working consistently at the borderline of architecture. The intention is to achieve new knowledge and inspiration from other design and construction disciplines. Transportation design is an ideal research topic in relation to micro architecture, as it combines the optimized use of minimal spaces with a high level of comfort, innovative technologies and lightweight materials. Growing environmental problems, the shortage of resources and the increasing demand on the flexibility of buildings are all adding greatly to the importance of lightweight structures in architecture.

As designers of lightweight structures, we are always looking for new ideas for saving resources both in the production and in the function of our projects. For all mobile objects a consistent lightweight construction has an impact, especially on the driving characteristics

this page:
Porsche 911 S;
Porsche 911 Turbo, interior

opposite page:
'Micro Bach';
Wally Sail 80, customized

PORSCHE

PORSCHE

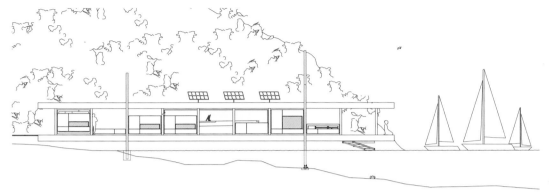

and the fuel consumption. There is hardly any other industry with such enormous expanse of research and development in this area as there is in transportation design. The development and use of new technologies, innovative materials, forms and joining techniques are characteristic of this research and represent the best thinking in more efficient building.

Though transportation design and architecture are two different disciplines, they have a number of issues in common to do with construction, production, assembly, aesthetics, emotions, ergonomics, sustainability and social aspects. A structure, a climate skin, storage, a customized interior design are elements that demonstrate the intersection of all of those concerns. Objects in both the fields of architecture and transportation are designed as a vision, tested and optimized on a virtual and haptic model, and then technically detailed to be built 1:1 as a final product. While a vehicle is built in a serial production of several thousand units, the

WALLY 143 Esense – Ph. Toni Meneguzzo

KS

architectural object is usually designed as a unique piece, though this is changing. For time and cost minimization, quality improvement and material efficiency, we are trying to develop micro architecture objects with a high degree of prefabrication and component design. There is a high potential in the processes and strategies of transportation design to enhance the building process in micro architecture. The emotional demands of the object as well as a clearly legible brand identity are particularly important to prevail on the market.

Micro architecture uses the human body and its ergonomics as the main reference for its scale in ways that are comparable to the interior design of a vehicle. In both cases the aim is to achieve maximum comfort for the user on minimal space. The sensitive combination of materials, surface design, form, colour and light can create a generous sense of space in a small area. How to optimize and reduce the required space is one of the leading questions we

this page:
'White Knight',
frontal view;
'Spaceshipone',
interior

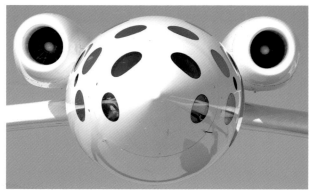

VIRGIN GALACTIC

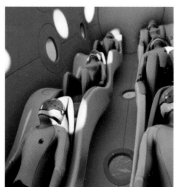

VIRGIN GALACTIC

78 | studio

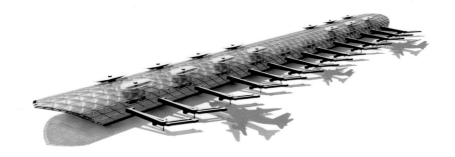

address at our Institute, and it is also relevant to sustainability.

Today, man spends most of his time in an artificially created space. At the Institute our intention is to regard the surrounding architecture not as a monument but as an instrument. Just like a car, an aircraft or a boat, the architecture should serve the user's needs at a high technical and aesthetic level.

Today, architecture and transportation collide in countless configurations. Totally new building typologies have been generated in the last hundred years or so in transportation hubs such as airports and railway stations. Does the architecture fit the transportation design?

In various design studios in our Institute, the students are urged to find inspiration and analogies in the field of transportation design.

The current semester at TUM deals with the design of a 'space-camp', a training centre and short-term residence for suborbital flight passengers with Virgin Galactic. For the diploma project in the winter term 2007/08, we asked the students to design a new terminal building for Munich Airport as a satellite facility. A small carbon boat, powered by alternative energies was the design task in 2006. Martin Francis, product designer and naval architect from London, and Gilberto Penzo, boat-building expert from Venice, were extremely helpful consultants for this task. The semester proceeded with such great success that we were invited to exhibit some of the results on the trade fair 'Boot 2007' in Düsseldorf.

Besides teaching, I am doing my PhD on 'micro architecture and transportation design, inspirations, analogies and potentials in lightweight structures', with the help of Prof. Richard Horden as doctoral adviser.

studio

dipl. ing. nadine zinser

habitation and transportation | 79

industry and architecture

Our Munich-based design studio has, among other advantages, that of location. We are situated not only a short distance from the Alps but very close to the headquarters, factories and design studios for very high-profile car and aeronautics companies such as BMW, Eurocopter and Schempp-Hirth. We are also close to industries linked to the Alps, for example, those who are involved in ski production or transportation systems, such as the company Doppelmayr. Technology transfer can have a great impact on advances in architecture. So, in our studio we not only keep abreast of advances in different industries that may be useful in our own research, but we try to develop architecture that asks industry to develop special techniques for certain projects. Every year we visit these cutting-edge firms with our students to learn as much as possible, focusing on, perhaps, the unique design language of a car, a plane or a helicopter and their respective interiors. These experiences have a direct effect on the students' thinking.

this page:
Map
Munich and industries
1 Kneissl – ski
2 Klepper – boats
3 Doppelmayr
4 Schempp-Hirth
5 Eurocopter
6 BMW

opposite page:
Design for a prefab
solar compact home
inspired by Doppelmayr

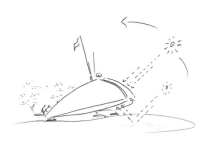

For example, students who spend more than a semester with us would never be content to choose a chair from the catalogue but would prefer to research their own unique furnishing solutions. In fact, in many cases we create fully integrated furniture for our projects rather than source ready-made types. In addition, our students also learn about colour control, composite materials, such as carbon, and, of course, lightweight structures. One result of our studies of technology transfer was the 'Solar Compact Home' (see page 262), which was developed in a logical sequence following the requirements of the project. A solar-cell manufacturer, who was invited for the final presentation, is now very interested in developing new solar cells with a high degree of efficiency which would also work as a waterproof skin for the double-curved shape of our building. When solar cells are finally so effective that they can use the energy of sunlight reflected by water, we will know that in this case we have asked the right questions.

dipl. ing. walter klasz

DOPPELMAYR

sport and architecture

It is no coincidence that most of the assistants in our micro architecture studio are involved in some kind of sport. Extreme alpine sporting activities, such as ice-climbing or windsurfing for example, give us the opportunity to experience nature in extraordinary ways. 'Don't fight forces but use them' is one of Buckminster Fuller's famous sayings. An ice-climber does not fight against the frozen cliffs, he uses the strength of the frozen water to fix his tools for some seconds and pull himself upward. During our last trip with the mobile 'Ski Haus' (see page 116) next to the Kleine Matterhorn (3,883m) we chose a frozen area for the new location of our temporary micro hotel. After we dug three small holes out of the ice, the helicopter could land the 'Ski Haus' on to those points, and a few hours later the feet had been frozen firmly to the site. With the structure's three feet embedded in the ice, Richard Horden and I felt quite secure inside, even during a heavy storm in the night.

this page:
'Ski Haus' – trip 2005, sunshine after the storm; ice-climber in Tyrol, nothing is left of the ice

opposite page:
merging with the board design project (above); surfer in Silvaplana; 'Event Centre', Silvaplana

WK

WK

We often explain to our students that developing architecture is similar to being involved in extreme sport. In the same way that a sportsman has to practice every day, you need stern discipline to achieve a really high level of performance in your designs. When we were working on the design of the temporary event centre, Silvaplana in Switzerland, the Institute had the feeling of a sport camp. The finished design of the centre was like a very effective piece of outdoors, or sporting, equipment that helps people to experience nature almost without having any impact on it. The three-point fixing allows the structure to be adjusted to any site; the shape creates a much-reduced contact surface against wind, and the large upper skin collects solar energy. When a surfer seems to merge with his surfboard, we look at it and instantly gain inspiration. When Norman Foster came to see the final presentation of the 'Event Centre' (arriving from St. Moritz on his lightweight racing bicycle), he was instantly moved.

dipl. ing. walter klasz

WK

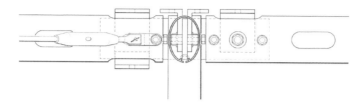

links and relationships

As a former student, then an architect for three years at Richard Horden's London-based office (Horden Cherry Lee Architects) and then teaching assistant at his TU Munich Institute for architecture and product design, I can reflect on Richard Horden's design ideas and strategies from three different viewpoints. During my studies we learned how to approach architecture in small scale. At this dimension you develop important skills, such as scrutinizing small details, which are also relevant to large-scale buildings. If you don't perfect the details, the concept for the whole building fails. Richard Horden's teaching is based on light structures and originates in yacht racing. As I am also a yachtsman I like the idea of using details from racing yachts, as they are aesthetically elegant, coming from a sport that has developed using high technology.

The base structure for the 'Yacht House' makes use of masts from sailing yachts. To connect these beams, Richard used a detail by the Californian Architect Raphael Soriano. He used

this page:
'Yacht House'
by Richard Horden,
Dorset, England;
IF design awarded
daysailor YSA-10
by Yacht designer
Sven Akermann

opposite page:
'Poole Waterfront
Museum', Horden
Cherry Lee Architects;
handrail detail at the
'Poole Waterfront
Museum' by UF

KK

TK

a flat plate in a cross shape to transfer the forces from the beam into the column head. It was a modification of this detail that was used for the 'Yacht House', which was built in the New Forest, England, in 1982. For the 'Waterfront Museum' in Poole harbour we used the language of maritime architecture. White steel beams continue the architectural form of the existing building with tall elegant arched steel frames that open towards the view over Poole Harbour. The plain and crisp style is continued into the detail of the handrail. In any part of design there is one concept, one style that continues the design into the detail to achieve a harmonious architecture. Another example of a strong architectural concept is 'Park Place' (see pages 10 and 12), an office building which expresses the reed bed nature of the Docklands before it was urbanized. Like a reed bed, Park Place also gains part of its energy for cooling from the deep geothermal piles that will be driven into the soft waterside and bedrock below.

TR

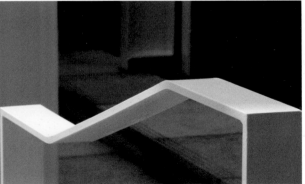

TR

carbon-fibre-reinforced plastic

For years we have been interested in using carbon-fibre-reinforced plastics as a regular building material. The advantages are simple and obvious: lightness and strength. Because we want to build light we cannot afford to overlook a material with these characteristics. However, there are disadvantages, the largest of these is cost. This is why carbon fibre is standard in high-tech yachts, aircraft, racing cars and all domains where weight matters and cost does not play such a crucial role. But why do we want to build light in regular, permanently fixed buildings of the usual dimensions? Lightweight construction means primarily a reduction in the mass of material used, which in turn results in a reduction in energy. This advantage was disregarded in the past, but now declining resources and rising prices for energy and raw materials make the lightweight aspect more important. But developing lighter buildings means more work for architects and engineers alike and it asks for a new cooperation between the two disciplines. The classical

this page:
carbon workshop,
winter semester
2007/08

opposite page:
students learning
different laminating
techniques

Carbon Workshop
09.-11.01.2008

role allocation is such that the architect designs the building and the engineer figures out how to make it stand up. But in the future, lightweight, sustainable structures will demand more from both. The architect needs a better understanding of the flow of forces, the characteristics of the material and the method of construction. The engineer will have to use his special knowledge in more creative ways. Some of the first experiments in lightweight structures that called for a more interdisciplinary cooperation were carried out by architects like Frei Otto. Later engineers such as Jörg Schlaich and Werner Sobek brought new ideas to the field. In our studio we want to spark greater interest in lightweight design and to find ways and techniques to use materials such as carbon-fibre-reinforced plastics in a more cost effective way and for a wider field of applications. To achieve this, we work hand in hand with the industry. Knowledge gained from this cooperation will be fed back to our students in teaching lessons and workshops which will continue to

ws ws ws

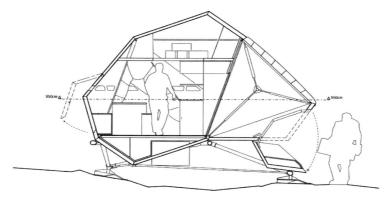

generate ideas about how to use the materials in new and unconventional ways. So that as industry informs our studies, our research may also produce advances in technology transfer well beyond our studio. **'Polar Lab'** In winter 2005/06 we developed, in cooperation with the Alfred Wegener Institute for Polar and Marine Research in Bremerhaven, a mobile research station for Antarctica. Four students were involved: Simone Hiesinger, Sandra Spindler, Michael Kehr and Eike Schling. The station is designed for transport by helicopter and accommodates a small team of scientists and all of their supplies for weeks at a time in an extremely cold climate. The geometry consists of eight equal-size sandwich panels in the form of asymmetric tetrahedrons. Together they form an octahedron, a Platonic solid composed of eight equilateral triangles. In this way a crystalline shape with an optimal proportion of volume and surface emerges with a very rigid structure and excellent aerodynamic properties. The eight panels are exchangeable and can therefore be produced in

this page:
'Polar Lab' photomontage and 1:1 mock-up

opposite page:
supported by the company Carbon Werke in Wallerstein we were able to build and test several panels in scale 1:1

SSp

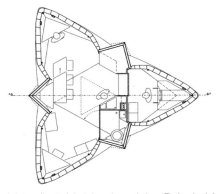

multiples very economically. The capsule rests on a height-adjustable tripod, and the 'Polar Lab' station weighs only 1.170kg, including the foot construction. It can be flown to its operational area with a conventional helicopter. Once deployed three of the eight panels can be unfolded and thus expand the volume of the capsule. When opened, the individually usable extensions, which are protected by an insulated membrane, expand the volume by 75 per cent and the usable floor area by 300 per cent. The sandwich elements are made from simple carbon-fibre sheets and a hard foam infill (thickness: 6cm). With a weight of only 7.5kg/m2 we achieve a heat transmission coefficient of 0.35w/m2k. Supported by the company Carbon Werke in Wallerstein we were able to build and test several full-scale panels. **'Aero Haus'** Another project was based on a design created in 1996 in collaboration with professor Helmut Richter at the Technische Universität Wien. The 'Fish Haus' (see page 156), as it was then called, is a bivouac that can be transported on the

(see page 156)

studio

dipl. ing. wieland schmidt

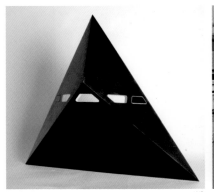

WS

WS

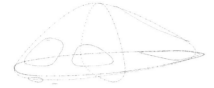

roof of a car. It stands on three supporting legs, with the car parked underneath if desired, then the legs can be folded up, allowing the car to drive away. Twelve years after the first models were made, we are building a full-size prototype with two students (Inga Mannewitz and Steffen Knopp). The first task in building the prototype was to generate a 3D model of the structure (now called 'Aero House'). We approached this issue in two different ways. Firstly, we used a micro scribe g2lx digitizer to gather single points on the surface, section and the location of the windows and openings. However, we were not completely satisfied with the 3D surfaces produced by these data. So we then scanned the complete model with an Atos high-end 3D digitizer to create an extremely precise 3D model. This flexible optical measuring device is based on the principle of triangulation. Projected fringe patterns are observed with two cameras and 3D coordinates for each camera pixel are calculated with high precision to generate a polygon mesh of the object's

this page:
gathering points with
a micro scribe g2lx
digitizer and scanning
the 'aero house' with
a high-end 3D digitizer
to create an extremely
precise 3D model

opposite page:
1:1 mock up and
1:1 prototype

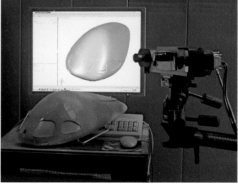

WS

IM

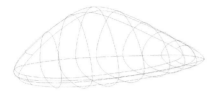

surface. From this scanned 3D model we generated a series of sections in three directions. To build the surface from these curves we used the plug-in t-spines for Rhino, a software tool that gives us optimal modelling control with machine precision and ensures full industry compatibility and seamless integration in the design process. Working in this way with the physical and digital models, we were able to generate a perfectly smooth and watertight surface that we can use for the next step: CNC milling a negative mould. Once that is achieved, we can produce several positive copies of the 'Aero House' by laminating a carbon-fibre-reinforced sandwich construction into the negative mould. The windows are vacuum-formed from separate positive CNC-milled models. The tripod construction will consist of custom-made 5cm-thick, carbon-fibre-reinforced tubes, similar to the mast of a sailboat. All of the carbon work will be executed in close cooperation with the same company who participated in the 'Polar Lab', Carbon Werke in Wallerstein.

studio

dipl. ing. wieland schmidt

SKn

IM

SKn

carbon-fibre-reinforced plastic | 91

in studio

At the commencement of one's studies at a university school of architecture a new world opens up, a discussion forum in which all manner of subjects are considered – tradition and modernism, abstraction and figurative deception, construction and fiction, as well as architecture itself, that most public of the arts. To retain control of a project as an architect, one has to learn how to play the central role as a coordinator of an interdisciplinary team, at the same time keeping sight of the universal work of art that is the architectural goal. Richard Horden, who was appointed professor at the University of Technology in Munich in 1996, founded the Microarchitecture Unit, Munich, in which design and its translation into reality is taught in close conjunction with professional practice. The concept is based on the implementation of micro-projects, which allow great control to be exercised over the design process and experience to be gained within a short time in what might be described as an 'architectural simulator'. From the very outset

this page:
mock-up of the
'i-home' in the studio

opposite page:
'Peak Lab' exhibition in
Zermatt, Switzerland;
design teams at the
'Trockener Steg' cable-
car station, 2,929m

WK   WK

students are urged to take account equally of the concept and its implementation, to work in a structured manner and to react swiftly to developments. The design tasks chosen for studies are often drawn from the realms of sport and leisure. In that respect, the special position and topography of the Munich area are very helpful, ranging from the high Alps to hilly and flat landscapes and including areas of water as well as urban developments. In other words, there is a wealth of leisure possibilities. As a result, students are better able to identify with their projects. In the words of Charles Eames: 'We take our pleasures seriously'.

(First published in *Detail* magazine, 12/04.)

WK

dipl. ing. lydia haack

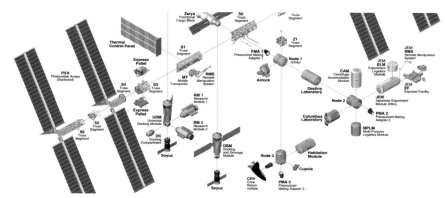

micro architecture and extreme environments

In 1998, two years after Richard Horden and I started teaching in Munich and had several key student projects like the 'Cliffhanger' and 'Beach Point' built, I thought we could do something a bit more exciting next. For me, the most exciting achievement of the last millennium was flying to space. As it happened, around this time the first modules for the International Space Station (ISS) were being prepared for launch and the ISS still had a dedicated 'Habitation Module'. Richard was excited when I proposed to him the idea for a Space Architecture semester. We quickly found professor of aerospace Eduard Igenbergs, who was very happy to work with architects and put the idea forward for 'humanized' spaceflight. It was Professor Igenbergs who brought us into contact with architect Hans Huber, inventor of the 1986 Munich Space Chair which later flew on the MIR. Further on we also worked closely with German astronaut Reinold Ewald, NASA and Constance Adams, as well as many other experts in the field. Equipped with

this page: the International Space Station in its early state

opposite page: section through the habitation module design by the students (above); the team from TU Munich performing hardware tests on parabolic flights with NASA in Houston

NASA

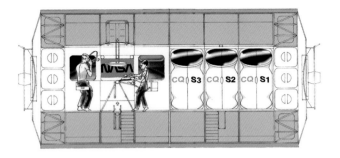

such a high-level teaching team we only lacked students for the course. Eventually we had seven participants, though a normal semester takes 40–50. However, the performance of these seven students was unparalleled. Within one year, from knowing virtually nothing about space and microgravity, they had designed, built and tested equipment for the habitation module of the ISS, which was successfully flown on parabolic flights out of NASA's Johnson Space Center in Houston. The students developed the interior of the habitation module by studying videos, taking aerospace classes, and talking to astronauts and engineers. The most important factor in their success, however, was the application of the architectural working method they had developed in Richard Horden's studio. Students started very early in the design process with models and mock-ups to understand the dimensions of the Habitation interior. This not only allowed them to comprehend the design problem, but also enabled them to get much more specific information

andreas vogler, dipl. arch eth

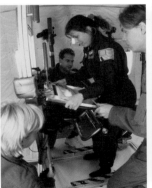

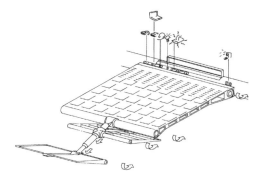

and comments from the experts. Especially valuable was the input from Constance Adams, a trained architect working in the space sector and at that time one of the architects responsible for the development of the TransHab module at NASA. The prototypes the students developed were far from science fiction but valuable contributions to future human spaceflight that not only impressed NASA experts, but nearly pushed their regular contractor out of business. However, although *Bayern Innovativ* financed the prototypes for TU Munich, at the time there was no agency or institution helping us to grasp this potential business opportunity. Later, the political situation in the US changed and the Habitation Module of the ISS was abandoned for cost reasons. At the TUM we continued the space projects with the planning for a Habitation module alongside NASA's Mars Reference Mission planning. The challenge of such a mission for the architect is to provide a home for six astronauts for nearly two years in a 7.5m-pressure vessel. Given all of the limita-

this page:
design prototype of the 'FLOW' workstation

opposite page:
crew quarter studies for a Mars habitation module (above); model of the Mars habitation module; interior view of a personal crew quarter in the Mars habitat

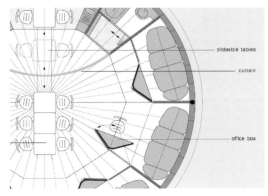

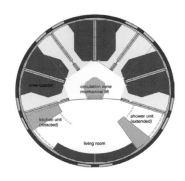

tions, constraints and unknowns of such a mission, public and private zones have to be planned on the tiniest spaces, allowing the astronauts not only to satisfy their physical requirements but also their personal psychological needs. In such an extreme, unforgiving and pioneering situation, architecture becomes the key integrator of safety, functionality and psychology. This not only requires the architect to have a fundamental grasp of engineering but also the ability to develop and verify concepts by scientific means. Space is the new frontier, but it has also proven to be a valuable field for teaching students the archetypal functions of architecture. In the absence of gravity many concepts and solutions we take for granted have to be reconsidered. The exposure to long-duration space exploration with its low energy availability and recycling requirements, makes us rethink our approach to terrestrial architecture. Only from space can the real beauty and also the fragility of our planet be seen and appreciated.

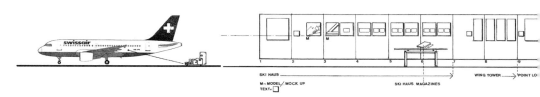

When I met Richard Horden first in the early 1990s he had already completed a considerable range of high-profile projects like the 'Yacht House' and 'Epsom Race Course'. He had just won the competition for the Wing Tower in Glasgow, the first tower to turn into the wind. However, the project he talked about with most enthusiasm was the little 'Ski Haus' (see page 116) in the Swiss Alps. For me, a student at the time, it was the first example of a built modern micro architecture. My colleague Jan Dvorak and I couldn't resist the desire to fly the 'Ski Haus' by helicopter into the campus of the ETH Zürich, where we were studying. For us, this was a wake-up call to the school still continuously praising the 'Swiss Box', that there is a whole new world of architecture to be explored. I doubt this was understood, for in Switzerland at the time architecture was big, square, concrete and plaster; certainly not micro, not triangular, not like a helicopter, not aluminium and definitely not fun. And we had a lot of fun with the 'Ski Haus'. Later, when I worked with

this page:
the 'Ski Haus' at the Eigerjoch, 3,720m; landing of the 'Ski Haus' at the campus of ETH Zurich for the exhibition opening

opposite page:
'Point Lookout', Bondi Beach, Sydney

AK

AV

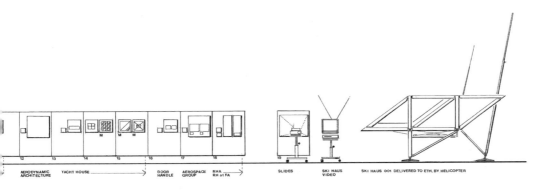

AERODYNAMIC ARCHITECTURE | YACHT HOUSE ——————→ | DOOR HANDLE | AEROSPACE GROUP | RHA RH at FA ——→ | SLIDES | SKI HAUS VIDEO | SKI HAUS 001 DELIVERED TO ETH. BY HELICOPTER

Richard Horden and he became professor at the TUM in Munich, it was clear we would take the 'Ski Haus' as a starting point for micro architecture studies with the students. The term micro architecture was not established with reference to architecture in those days; it was primarily used in information technology. However, since then several books about small architecture have come on the market and well-respected magazines, like *Detail*, have devoted several issues to micro architecture. It has become a serious field for many clients and young architects. But what is micro architecture? Is it just small buildings? No, it is not. It is primarily about nature and people enjoying nature. Even if the structure is mobile, the idea is to create a temporary place, to touch the Earth lightly. It is about a see-through and transparent architecture, architecture that enhances the beauty of nature without compromising it. It is not about 'bricks on wheels' as Richard Horden calls common caravans, or 'potatoes on sticks', or 'putting lipstick on a gorilla'. The beauty of

RH

RH

micro architecture and extreme environments | 99

nature is also the key to our involvement with extreme environment. It is the respect for nature and the very needs of the people living and working there that are the generators of this micro architecture, not technology or the aim to achieve something high-tech. This is something students have to learn. Technology, structure, materials, transportation have all to be developed during the design process to provide the client with a viable product, but this is always done in the context of enhancing the place and creating something beautiful. As architecture becomes smaller, like the size of a car or an aeroplane, it comes closer to the people who are meant to use it. Materials and details become more important and require more attention. Structure and surface become one. This makes a perfect study object for educating young architects. The scale of the projects also means that over the course of one year, students go through the whole design process, from concept to design definition, to detailing, mock-up development and production. They are

this page: typical student drawings (above); full-size proto-types and scale model from the micro architecture design studio

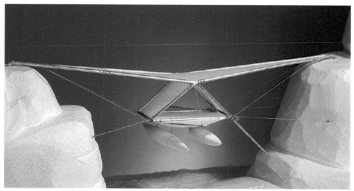

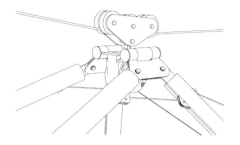

involved in communication with experts, fund-raising and publication of the built projects. Many of the students who have gone through this programme have probably learnt more about the process of architecture and design than in any other design studio.

Recently, my office partner Arturo Vittori and myself had the pleasure of being invited as critics to the studio run by Richard Horden, and after teaching in many places all over the world, I am still amazed to see the high level of design quality this studio is achieving right from the start. However, there is no magic behind it. There is a nice atmosphere, a friendly and dedicated teaching team, a sense of precision and discipline as you would expect in a good design office. If you go to the studio, you find students sketching up ideas, drawing, building models and mock-ups. But there is such a sense of excitement and inspiration, as if they know they are achieving something great even if it is small in size!

space projects

'Hans Huber is an architect and product designer now advising an automotive supplier. He designed the original 'Space Chair' in the 1980s at the TUM. This was tested on the MIR Space Station and now on the International Space Station. He guided our teams on the development of the Astronaut Work station and other NASA projects'   RH

Micro architecture is essential for extreme environments. The more extreme the environment, the smaller the hull you can afford to build and to transport in order to protect the human being. In a high-tech environment like the International Space Station (ISS) only two cubic metres of private space are available for each astronaut. So you have to design the hull very carefully to fulfill all the needs of its inhabitants. In extreme environments you also have to plan waste management and supply, as nothing works in the ways you are accustomed to. For example, nothing rots in the Arctic. You have to cope with this and use technologies that differ from those that might be used in a temperate environment. In space the designer must deal with additional problems due to weightlessness. The neutral position of the human body in weightlessness is different from that at normal gravity, and that means the requirements for a workstation in space are different. Fixation is necessary in 0g. Without it you are not able to use both hands. Known solutions such as foot loops have specific disadvantages, for example, to do with lower-leg muscle fatigue. So, starting with the neutral position in 0g, I designed the Munich Space Chair (MSC). It enables the users to work with both hands while being comfortably secured in the chair at the waist position. This also enables the upper body to move with the agility to perform various precise tasks. This is important because an astronaut's time is so precious and costly in space, so an efficient means of working while being comfortably held in place is vital to the speed, precision and success of the research being carried out. The space department of the TUM, at that time headed by Prof. Dr.-Ing. Eduard Igenbergs, used the concept of my MSC to develop the hardware for flight testing. The MSC was sent aboard the MIR space station in 1995 and was used there by the German astronaut Thomas Reiter. In August 2007 it was sent to the ISS, and usage and experiments started there in March 2008.

People do not usually go to extreme environments for leisure but because they are engaged in some kind of work, conducting experiments, doing research and so on. So as a designer you have to provide a workplace that is as good as possible in the circumstances. However, the more extreme the environment, the harder it is to create a really good habitat, i.e. micro architecture, around the workplace. These limitations are not only relevant in extreme climates but in extreme industrial environments, such as in some areas of the construction industry. This is a field in which many interesting and very technical tasks await architects. In addition to harsh industrial environments such as foundries, a lot of new extreme conditions have developed in industry during the last decades, for example on oil rigs, in clean-rooms and in advanced robotic automobile factories. The workplaces in these environments should also be as excellent as possible, and designing them is an important challenge for architects in the future.

studio

dipl. ing. hans huber

knowledge transfer

As a teacher at a university architecture department I am often dealing with questions like, 'what is complex 3D conceptual design?', and 'how do we communicate it?'. The study of these questions is producing a huge variety of complex spatial ideas. In developing designs many different aspects have to be considered such as functional, constructive and creative parameters. These different requirements for the design cannot be executed step by step; they involve overlap and interlock. The method of resolution for such tasks requires a certain integral 'concurrency'. Naturally young students cannot immediately cope with this complexity, so many aspects have to be factored out in the initial stages. Still, the consequences of basic decisions in the conceptual design are not always obvious, for instance those concerning human factors. The flaws in the original concept may only show up much later in the design and production process. Richard Horden approaches the teaching of architecture in another way. He prefers to offer small and unconventional tasks that

this page:
student project 2001
'Carbon-fibre House',
M. Pektor, C.
Roettinger
opposite page:
student project 2004
art lab (above),
P. Sturmhofer
J. Pietraszewski;
student project 2000
living scape, H. Friese,
D. Payer

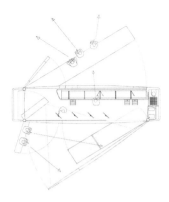

cross the border between product design and architecture to lead to sustainable and adaptable architectural concepts. Students learn to create a conceptual design continuously from detail through to the completion of the entire form. Understanding architecture as a product helps them to loosen former cultural fixes and established ideas of architecture. Classically, architecture is primarily concerned with creating a unique, one-off prototype, while product design is intended for mass production and duplication from the beginning, and is therefore more concerned with issues of weight, transport and methods of production. Traditionally built architecture has a predetermined function at a certain place; it is fixed and relates to a defined environment. Products are developed for different situations at different places. The design process for the students is thereby defined by iterative development as it is within product design. Using an analytical approach to find new, effective concepts has become the architectural challenge of our time.

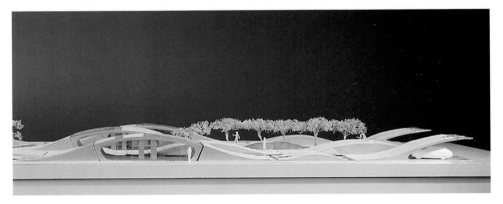

Tasks related to the field of product design are also a very important topic at Lehrstuhl für drei-dimensionales Gestalten (Three Dimensional Design), at TU Vienna. However, the focus is slightly different, and our main concern is to deal with complex geometries which are a matter of course in product design for ergonomic and stylistic reasons. New analysis and computer programmes have also inspired more complex forms in architecture, so that soon rectangular geometric restrictions will no longer be the accepted norm in the built environment. Product designers create their own illustrative techniques and proceedings for complex geometries and even their own linguistic and semantic repertoire. This know-how can also be used by architects to produce more open forms and to control them. Computer software simplifies the production of such new forms at first but their quality can only be proved and evaluated in physical reality. Computer-controlled manufacturing methods such as milling and cutting techniques, and stereoscopic prints offer the

this page:
digitizer, micro scribe gx2 (above); student project 2008, 'secret form', B. steiner, R. steffek

opposite page:
7 axis milling robot kuka kr 60 ha (above); student project 2008, 'secret form', E. Hofstetter, S. schopf

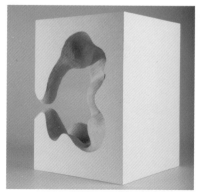

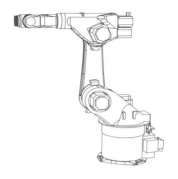

ability to create physical samples out of virtual, computer-generated samples. For this purpose we are establishing with the appropriate equipment, the 'v2r-lab' (virtuality to reality laboratory). The sample object produced in this workshop should not only represent a fixed form at its final stage, it should also function as a working model still open for changes. Therefore we are designing a computer-controlled foam-laying machine at present. This will give the students the opportunity to produce quick models to be worked over manually and to explore different shapes during the design process. To integrate manual and CNC manufacturing techniques we use 3D laser scanners to feed manually worked-over models back into the digital design. The students will then be confronted with the file-to-factory process in which their own drawings will be used directly to produce units. These techniques will be increasingly important for creative control and for the realization of complex geometries both in academic situations and in architectural practice.

studio

prof. christian kern

 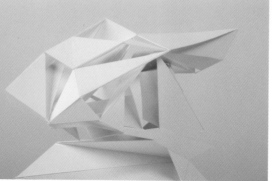

art and architecture

When we write about art and architecture, either the art or the architecture comes first. In an ideal world the architecture becomes a bit of art and art becomes a bit of architecture: the two are allowed to enhance and not compete with one another. In order for this to occur the architecture and the art have to 'fit' each other. A 'light' architectural space usually requires a 'light' artwork, since placing a 'heavy' artwork there would result in an alteration of the space. Another element is scale. Art requires its own space. If, for example, an artwork is crammed into a space, the architectural space either seems unable to accommodate the artwork or the artwork itself seems out of proportion in relation to the space it occupies.

Blurring the line between art and architecture does not always require a deep understanding of the meaning of place, space and site. It does require a sense of these elements, so the boundaries between the two can be acknowledged and treated as desired. Art comes first from

this page:
Cube necklace; the
Mermaid Bridge,
Auckland, NZ

opposite page:
'Reed Huis'

AMJ

RH

the heart and from intuition and secondly from the use and awareness of lines, space and the various illusions implicit in them. An example of art and architecture can be seen in my Mermaid Bridge at the Farm Sculpture Park near Auckland, New Zealand. This is composed of a series of large frame-cubes which I also use at a very small and precise scale for the composition of jewelry. For me it is a delicate step to link tiny frame-cubes together to create a piece of jewelry which I call 'sculpture for the body' or to create a bridge 'jewelry for the landscape'.

Another example of the crossover and interdependence of art and architecture is the 'Reed Huis' an adaption of the micro compact home ['m-ch'] using my reed sculptures. The composition is like a bird's nest held by the reeds. The micro compact home represents mass and density and the reeds openness and transparency. The small gentle cube appears to float by itself, with the corners clearly expressed using the three-point support from the reeds. Richard

EO

Horden and I designed the 'Reed Huis', adapting the design of the 'm-ch' and my sculptures. One of my reed sculptures consists of three gently curving vertical tubes, so we incorporated these essential elements of the sculpture with those for the 'm-ch' to create a balance between art and architecture. Both the sculptures and the little 'Reed Huis' benefit by a reduction to three shared supports.

micro architecture | projects

contents

Munich, Zurich, Lucerne and Chur are all cities within the 'Alpine Ring' and a one-hour drive from 3,000m peaks, so all are excellent locations for our micro architecture studies in the Alps. The collaboration between students, assistants and professors at these different schools has sparked some of the most varied and innovative projects. Our guiding principle is to 'touch the mountain lightly' meaning to arrive and leave with the mountain nature least disturbed and with the minimum of energy use for construction and installation. Ironically the helicopter offers a relatively low-energy option for transport to otherwise inaccessible locations, providing the elements of the building are designed for that method of delivery. It takes approximately 15 minutes to deliver a weight of 700 kilos from 1,600m to 4,000m i.e., the weight of the 'ski haus' or one component part of the 'peak lab' project lifted from Zermatt to the Kleines Matterhorn. Prof. Ulrich Pfammatter was based at HTA Lucerne and HTW Chur and enabled some remarkable projects with us through his connections to the Town Hall organizations and Swiss Alpine Club in Zermatt and Silvaplana near St. Moritz.

ski haus I cliffhanger I silva spider I white water I

'touch the earth lightly'

mountains

I fly off I peak lab I peak lab 02 I event centre silvaplana 01 I event centre silvaplana 02

Kleines Matterhorn (left) and Weisshorn (centre) from the 'ski haus' at 3,980m

RH

ski haus

Developed by Richard Horden and two of his students in Philadelphia in 1992, the 'ski haus' is the prototype of all micro-architecture projects that followed. This 'all-time classic' has now been in use for 15 years. In April 2004 the 'ski haus' was installed with the helicopter in its new location near the Matterhorn. Since then, it has been visited several times by Richard Horden or members of the Institute – and by many unknown mountain climbers on their way from Kleines Matterhorn to Breithorn. The 450kg structure consists of a loadbearing framework of yacht-mast sections. Three adjustable feet allow it to be erected on almost any terrain. Inside the 'ski haus', there is space for four people to sleep on tubular aluminium bunks. Two comfortable seats at the front also afford a panoramic view of the natural surroundings when the weather is fine. Today, the 'ski haus' is used as emergency accommodation or as a mobile station for high-altitude research.

WK

'ski haus' at installation in 'swizzaly', 14.04.04 (Swiss-Italian border at Gobba di Rollin, 3,899m)

Students	Ken Boyd	**Mountain Guide**	Marco Bomio
	Brian Kelly	**Helicopter Pilot**	Daniel Brunner
Teaching Team	Richard Horden	**Photographer**	Alex Kallenberger
	Sarah Kirby	**Sites**	Eigerjoch, 3,720m aod
			Gwächtejoch, 3,102m aod
			ETH Hönggerberg, Zürich, 525m aod
		Current Site	Gobba di Rollin, 3,901m aod, Zermatt

design team

Red paint on the components avoids loss in snow. Small pin joints are wired to the frame for security.

'ski haus' has a basic wind speed and direction indicator, an altimeter, a thermometer and a radio.

The three nicad batteries are charged from solar cells mounted horizontally.

The first high location of the 'ski haus' was on the Eigerjoch at 3,720m. Guide Marco Bomio is preparing fixings to the glacier ice.

RH

The legs of the 'ski haus' can be folded up to adapt it to ground conditions and for road transportation.

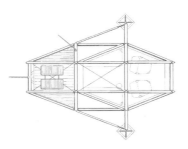

Plan of the 'ski haus' showing the solar panels on the roof.

AK

Project	Munich, 1997	**Sponsorship**	Alu Meier, Munich
Location	Lake Garda, Italy		Müller Design Technik,
Students	Alexander Felix		Hardheim
	Christopher		Beilken, Lemwerder
	von der Howen	**Materials**	Aluminium, Canvas,
Teaching Team	Eva Neumeyer		Plastimesh sheet
	Andreas Vogler	**Dimensions**	4.10 x 3.38m
	Prof. Richard Horden	**Weight**	36kg
Consultants	Tim Brengelmann,		
	Structural Design		
	Prof. R. Barthel, TUM		

design team

cliffhanger

'Cliffhanger' was designed as a platform for surfers, yachts-people and climbers on Lake Garda in Italy, which is three hours by car south of Munich. Designed to be suspended only a few metres above the water, it is conceived as a place for resting and sunbathing, and as an observation point for regattas. The extreme location on a sheer rock wall as well as difficult conditions of transport and assembly necessitated a minimal, lightweight form of construction without any great technical elaboration. Two tubular members are connected at one end to form a V-shape and are braced by two members that have the cross-section of a yacht mast. The structure is stayed by 'Dyneema' cables fixed to two pitons in the rockface. A glass-fibre-reinforced synthetic mesh stretched between the tubes provides a deck for sitting and reclining. Additional comfort is provided by a sunshade sail – which can be unfolded to form a tent – and by a sack for further equipment.

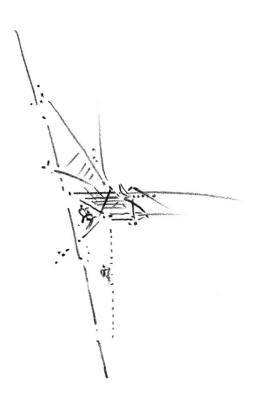

silva spider

Spiders have conquered every corner of our planet. Tremendously adaptable, they find a foothold everywhere, whether on their own legs or suspended in their self-built webs. This inspired the concept of the 'silva spider'. The aluminium structure, with three fully movable legs, is resolved into compression and tension members, in accordance with the principle of tensegrity. 'Silva spider' can, therefore, accommodate itself to any topography and will find a firm footing even in gorges and in gaps between buildings. A glass-fibre-reinforced plastic cabin with a mouldable aluminium honeycomb core and acrylic glass window elements is inserted in the structure. In an open position the flaps in the sides provide protection against the sun and afford an unimpeded view. A photovoltaic coating on the outside of the flaps generates energy for the cell.

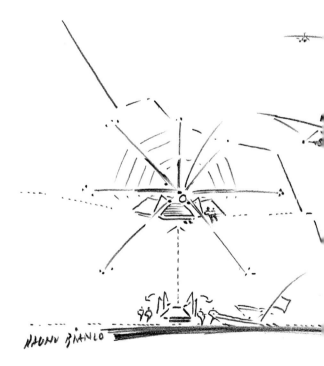

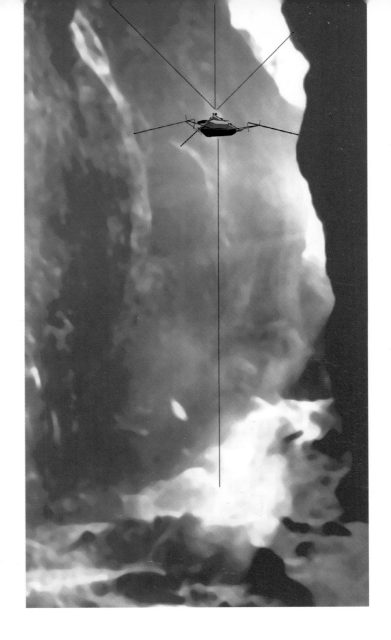

Project	Munich, 1997	**Consultants**	Tim Brengelmann, Dept. for
Location	Partnachklamm,		Structural Design
	Garmisch-Partenkirchen		Prof. R. Barthel, TUM
Students	Jürgen Amann	**Materials**	Aluminium,
	Thomas Wenig		Glass-reinforced plastic (grp)
Teaching Team	Andreas Vogler	**Dimensions**	2.3 x 2.3 x 1.4m
	Prof. Richard Horden	**Weight**	130kg

design team

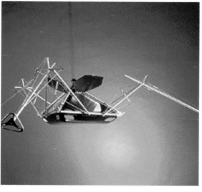

The 1:5 model, with a cabin for two people integrated into the tensegrity structure.

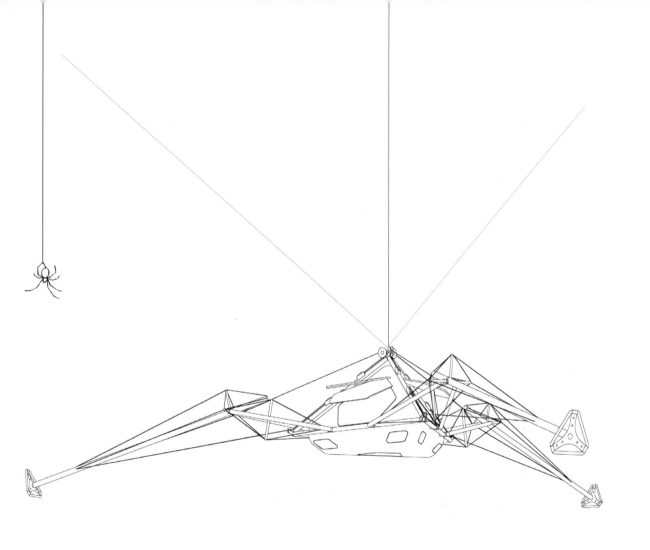

Project	Munich, 1998	**Consultants**	Tim Brengelmann, Dept. for
Location	River Ammer,		Structural Design
	near Saulgrub		Prof. R. Barthel, TUM
Students	Katrin Doll	**Materials**	Aluminium, Canvas
	Sabine Frohmader	**Dimensions**	12 x 1.2 x 1.4m
	Christina Reschke	**Weight**	100kg
	Claudia Wieshuber		
Teaching Team	Craig Synnestvedt		
	Prof. Richard Horden		

design team

white water

The river Ammer offers one of the most interesting stretches of white water for canoeists in the foothills of the Bavaian Alps. At one point, the rock walls on both sides form a natural gateway that leads to a long stretch of rapids, accessible only by kayak. The 'white water' project highlights this special situation. The narrows are spanned by a lightweight structure that acts as a bridge, as a viewing platform and as a place to spend the night. Canoeists can pull their boats out of the water and climb up the rockface by means of metal rungs. A cable system fixed to the frame structure allows kayaks to be hung beneath the bridge. A set of sails can be unfolded if required to create a protected space in which to spend the night.

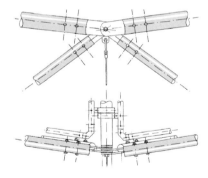

Simple pin-joint details facilitate easy assembly.

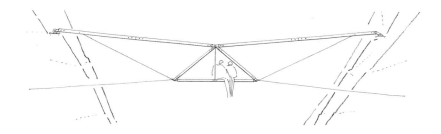

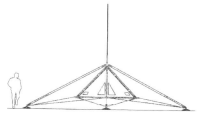

fly off

Inspired by the hang-glider, a team of two students guided by pilot and coaching assistant Andreas Vogler developed a tent for high mountain regions which is lifted above the snow on a light aluminium frame. Like the 'ski haus' the triangular feet of the frame can be inserted in a shallow recess in the ice and backfilled to make a secure fixing even in the high-altitude winds. The project involved structural engineering and careful detailing to produce an effective lightweight structure using 40mm tubing. The 26 detailed construction drawings contained some of the best technical work which we have seen at the TU Munich and the detailing continued in the plate and tube jointing concept which we had carried over from the 'yacht house' project in the New Forest in England in 1982 (see page 307). The project was constructed and taken to the Zugspitze for site testing and has been used for demonstration to our students of IBT (International Building Technologies).

1:1 construction
detail at the
Zugspitze

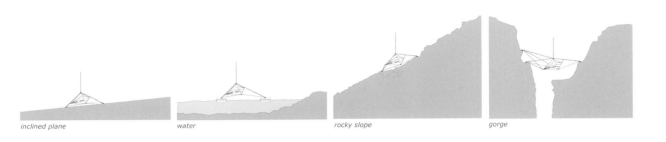

inclined plane   water   rocky slope   gorge

Project Munich, 2001
Location Alps
Students Clemens Bachmann
Michael Stoppe
Teaching Team Prof. Richard Horden

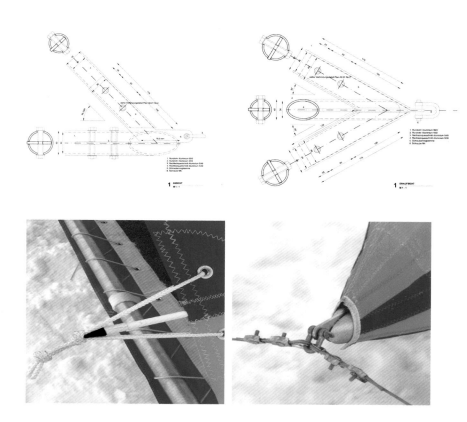

peak lab

'Peak lab' is a forward-looking, interdisciplinary and international model for the
combination of teaching and research.
For this project architectural students
from Lucerne and Munich as well as
mechanical engineering students from
the HTA Lucerne worked together on
a very complex conceptual formulation
and everybody profited from the different competencies, experiences and
backgrounds of the others. The aim
of the project is to develop a spacious
attractive 'camp', using light construction methods, which includes areas for
working and living, has self supply and
disposal, is simple to mount and de-
mount, and has a self-sufficient energy
supply. And it should do these things in
the extreme climate of 4,000m on the
Kleines Matterhorn, near Zermatt. This
extreme situation with its extraordinary
conditions requires just such new and
innovative solutions. Prefabrication is
necessary since it is only possible to
build in this high alpine region for 50
days of the year. Factory assembly
also guarantees a high standard of

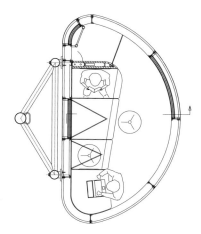

the manufacturing precision and less pollution produced during difficult site construction.

The vertical stratification of the 'peak lab' combines several advantages. The risks of rock-falls and snowdrifts are minimized, and there are aerodynamic benefits to the design. The site is also perfect for a vertical structure in other ways. The rock stands at an almost 90-degree angle, with the sun shining against it for most of the day. Direct sunlight is a very important element in this project because all of the power is generated by solar cells. These cells are evaporated directly on to the skin and are formative to the appearance of the building. Access to the building is from a small path that leads down from an observation platform at the top of the mountain. Finally this high-tech, low-impact facility offers wonderful views to the Breithorn and the Gobba di Rollin.

The horizontal and vertical dimensions of the 'peak lab' are very small, the available space has to be used in

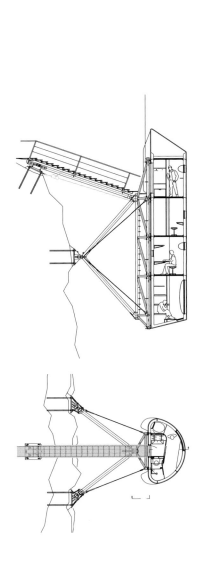

Project	Lucerne / Munich, 2002–03	**Teaching Team**	Prof. Richard Horden
			Prof. Ueli Pfammatter
Location	Kleines Matterhorn, Zermatt		Christian Fierz
			Mathias Frey
Students	Yann Friedl, Felix Häusler		Lydia Haack
	Christian Heck, Christine		Walter Klasz
	Neumann, Florian Uhl		Armando Meletta
	Vitus Erni, Stefan	**Consultants**	Prof. Joseph Schwartz
	Gassmann, Daniel		Prof. Urs Rieder
	Schatzmann, Christian		
	Schmidiger, David		
	Schneeberger		

design team

an optimal way. So the human scale was decisive for the design of the interior. The space for movement depends on the dimensions of the human body with certain lengths and radii of its extremities. The basic shape of the furniture is deliberately asymmetric in order to widen some spaces and provides zones for movement. Just like the single modules, which are stacked to create the 'peak lab', the furniture hangs backwards on a supporting system. It is mobile, so each room can be used for various activities. A ladder connects the modules vertically, in keeping with the principle of climbing on the mountain. The cliff-side façade is opened partially and offers views to the rock.

shell build up

3mm aluminium sheet
3cm air gap
3cm rohacell
3cm microtherm
3cm microtherm

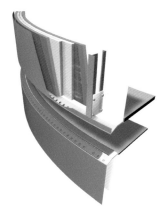

<table>
<tr><td rowspan="6">design team</td></tr>
</table>

Project	Munich, 2003	**Teaching Team**	Prof. Richard Horden
Location	Zermatt, Switzerland		Prof. Ueli Pfammatter
Students	Peter Böhm		Christian Fierz
	Ulrike Fuchs		Lydia Haack
	Christian Neubauer		Walter Klasz
	Michael Smola	**Consultants**	Andreas Orgler, Architect
			Innsbruck, Austria

peak lab 02

This is a modular designed mountain lodge, situated in the breathtaking panorama of the summits around Zermatt, Switzerland. It is conceived as a research and test centre for modern mountain equipment. The long horizontal shape of the building arises from the idea of zooming in visually on one of the most prominent peaks in the Alps, the Matterhorn. The building is arranged like a big telescope that focuses on the sharp, isolated rock pyramid with its steep narrow ridges jutting from surrounding glaciers. Sitting almost at the top of the Kleines Matterhorn on a ridge in the south-east, the building consists of eight modules – each 2.40 x 3.50 x 2.50m – and is created to meet minimal habitation requirements in an extreme environment. The site at almost 4,000m altitude makes exceedingly great demands on the building structure. Construction is only possible by means of prefabrication and helicopter support. But the result is that demands on the natural site are minimal.

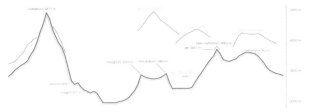

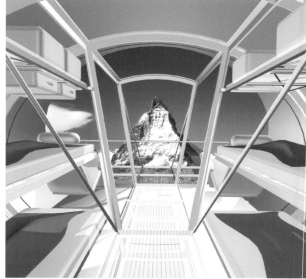

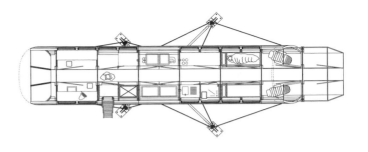

design team				
Project	Event Centre Silvaplana, 2006	**Teaching Team**	Prof. Richard Horden, TUM
Location	Summer/Lake Silvaplana Winter/Skiresort Corvatsch		Prof. Ueli Pfammatter, HTW Chur
Students	Henry Rist		Wieland Schmidt
	Sebastian Uhl	**Consultants**	Cajetan Piaget
	Fabio Wendnagel		Project assistant, Coordination at Chur

event centre silvaplana 01

The purpose of this event centre is to provide space and shelter for the jury of a surf- or snowboard-race, for award ceremonies or press events. The main shape of the structure was inspired by two inflated parachutes. They will be the only closed elements, ensuring a maximum of transparency through and out of the project. Yet the simple form is also eye-catching, and offers great potential for a corporate identity. The beautiful landscape is preserved around an object that does not only touch the ground lightly but also hardly affects nature underneath it. The modular construction allows for a simple assembly starting with the foot framework followed by the middle beam module that supports the whole static system. Due to its light weight and size (not more than 5 x 2m), transportation is possible by lorry or helicopter.

Norman Foster attended the students presentation on Lake Silvaplana close to St. Moritz.

structure
insulated shell
solar panels

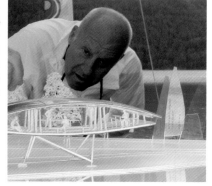

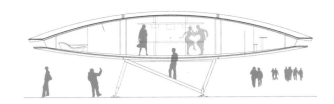

design team

Project	Event Centre Silvaplana, 2006	**Teaching Team**	Prof. Richard Horden, TUM Prof. Ueli Pfammatter, HTW Chur
Location	Summer/Lake Silvaplana Winter/Skiresort Corvatsch		Nadine Zinser Walter Klasz
Students	Annegret Lochbrunner Jerome Anton Daniel Castilla Toledo	**Consultants**	Cajetan Piaget Project assistant, Coordination at Chur
		Materials	Aluminium, ETFE Pillows
		Weight	3.20t

event centre silvaplana 02

An analysis of extreme sports reveals that their attraction is in providing an escape from daily life and the experience of nature and a feeling of lightness, for example, when skiing. These aspects are the key attributes for this design, an upside-down tetrahedron. Its main space is elevated from the ground and can be used as work or conference space or as a lounge for social events. The façade is made out of ETFE-pillows (translucent plastic membrane) and works as a printable advertisement space which can be easily altered. The surface can then be lit from inside, enhancing the building's character as a crystalline geometric artifact. The completed structure weighs 3.20t only and can be transported to a desired site by helicopter.

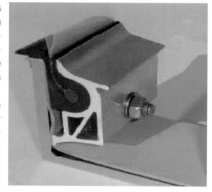

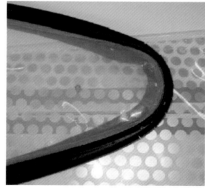

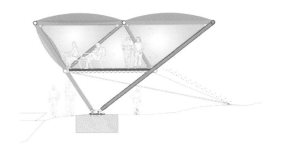

Watersides offer unique qualities for design that make them fascinating topics for study of both micro and macro architecture. Sun and sky light are reflected off the water surface creating a different illumination which can create a moving, dappled light on ceilings and an up-light onto façades which is so special to the location; this reflected up-light can also enhance the solar energy gain for a waterside situation. In addition the building or structure is reflected in the vibrant surface when viewed offshore. Vertical architecture is a characteristic of the lagoons of Venice but also in elegant waterside cities like Amsterdam and Copenhagen. The traditional buildings there have tightly spaced timber piles to distribute the weight of the stone buildings into the soft mud and sand substrate and so the spans on the upper levels must also be tightly spaced. This creates the charming verticality that we associate so much with Venetian and Dutch urban architecture. This special characteristic is also seen in the vertical piles that restrain the gondolas, *sandolo* fishing boats, Riva launches, water taxis and *vaporettos* of the Serenissima. Verticals reflect well in the water surface, and allow the boats to rise and fall with the short chop wave characteristic of San Marco. We always guide our students towards verticality for the waterside. We also bring ideas, which we have learnt so well with our students from our annual visits to Venice – Munich is a 40-minute flight away, to our London river and dockside architecture as well as to the wonderful micro architecture projects in Australia and California illustrated in the following pages.

Venetian Gilberto Penzo, is the author of the book *The Gondola* and builds the most beautifully accurate cherry-wood models of *gondolinos* (racing gondola) and *sandolos*, as well as of the other 100 or so types of boat in the city's history. Every year I visit his workshop in St. Thomas in the maze of tiny streets that make that part of the city and enjoy the precision of his work and the breadth of his knowledge. Gilberto came to Munich to guide the students in their boat-design projects together with Martin Francis, an architect and yacht designer from London who created the fastest and one of the most elegant private yachts ever produced.

waterside

point lookout | beach point | fish haus | carbon-fibre house | kayak club | loch ness | serenissima |
summer art school | 'iPod'™ house |

Lake Mackenzie on Frazer Island, Australia

RH

point lookout

'Point lookout' is an aluminium and acrylic canvas 'beach rig' and lifeguard's station, which provides a raised viewing platform and shade canopy with an integral high-level tent to use as a bivouac in remote locations. The rig was designed and built for a student architectural conference in the Mount Lofty Range, South Australia, to explore lightweight 'micro architecture' in 1993. The complete aluminium frame weighs approximately 70kg which makes it easy to transport. Assembly takes about one hour. Large triangular aluminium foot plates spread the download over soft sand or coral locations. Heights and levels are adjustable, as with a photographic tripod. The fabric is acrylic canvas; the tent is in 'rip stop' nylon. The frame is coated with high-strength, marine quality paint. Rope-work forms a second level of space enclosure and controls the canopy, the seat angle and overall adjustability.

RH

'Point lookout' is designed to be used by explorers, camera crews etc. in remote locations, as well as by lifeguards and surfers on beaches where permanent constructions are not permitted. Several 'point lookouts' might form a temporary 'sailboard village' for race meetings.

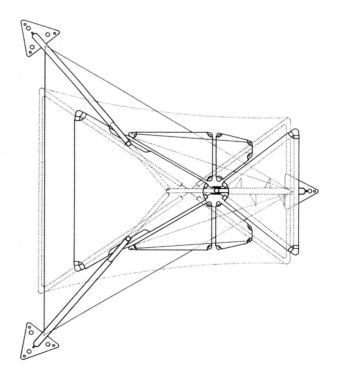

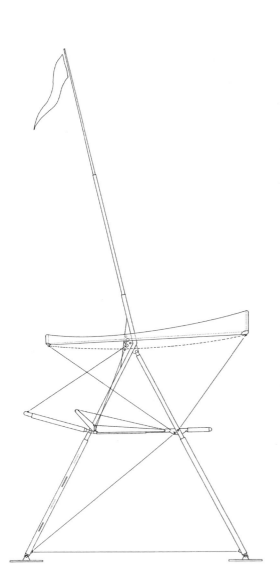

Project	England, 1993	**Materials**	Aluminium, Canvas
Location	Formula Spears, Lymington	**Weight**	70kg
Students	Scott Read		
	Russell Jones		
	Bill Cuneo		
	Andy Edwards		
	Chris Exner		
	Sarah McCarthy		
Teaching Team	Prof. Richard Horden		

design team

The platform of 'point lookout' sleeps two people. More hammocks can be attached below. The raised platform and shade canopy can be adjusted in height. Further camping equipment like mosquito nets, barbecues etc., can be attached to the platform.

RH

RH

beach point

'Beach point' is a mobile observation tower with a deck and two elevated seats. The idea is based on existing rescue stations on the Bavarian mountain lakes and is also a development of 'point lookout'. The finished structure has been used as far away as the beaches of California. All components are limited to a maximum length of four metres and a maximum total weight of 180kg. Packed in three boxes, they can be carried by two people to relatively inaccessible locations. Simple connections, based on boat construction details, allow the structure to be quickly assembled. The need for great stability even under extreme wind conditions necessitated comprehensive wind-tunnel tests, on which the structural calculations were based. By the success of this project, the students set up their own design office under the name 'microsystems'.

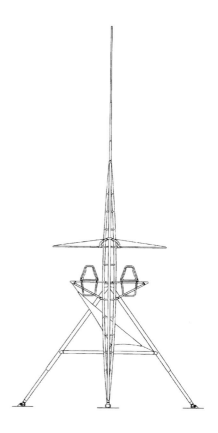

Students on the 'beach point' during a press event on Laguna Beach, California.

design team		
Project	Munich, 1997	**Consultants**	Tim Brengelmann,
Location	Walchensee, Germany,		Dept. for Structural Design,
	Laguna Beach,		Prof. Reiner Barthel, TUM
	California, USA		Prof. Albert Peripeintner,
Students	Jürgen Schubert		Dept. for Fluid Mechanics,
	Peter Zimmer		Prof. Boris Laschka, TUM
	Thorsten Schwabe	**Materials**	Aluminium
	Markus Kottermeier	**Dimensions**	4.30 x 4.80 x 10m
Teaching Team	Prof. Richard Horden	**Weight**	180kg
	Lydia Haack		

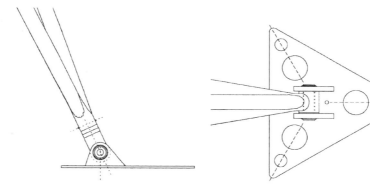

Details of the powder-
coated aluminium struc-
ture with integrated
canvas platform and
sunshade sail.

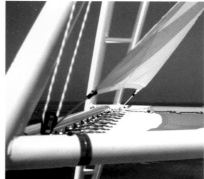

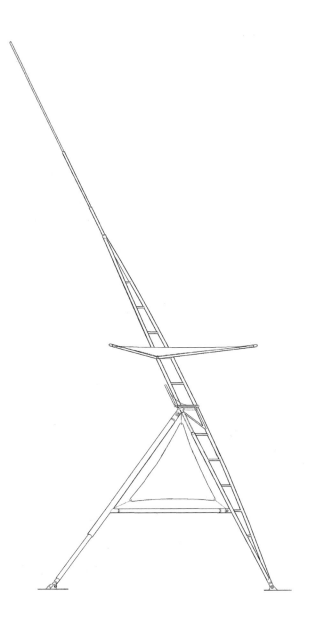

design team				
Project	Vienna, 1996		**Teaching Team**	Prof. Richard Horden
Location	Vienna			Andreas Vogler
Students	Gerhard Abel			Willi Frötscher
	Ursula Hammerschick			Anne Wagner
	Silvia Hörndl		**Consultants**	Prof. Helmut Richter,
	Martin Janecek			University of Technology
	Brigitta Kunsch			Vienna
	Paul Linsbauer			
	Christopher Lottersberger			
	Michael Quixtner			
	Magrit Rammer			

fish haus

The project was first developed with a team of nine students at the TU Vienna in 1996. Andreas Vogler and I asked students to visit the Fishermen's houses built on the grassed banks of the Danube and develop a project informed by these huts. They are raised above the ground to protect them from flooding. We titled the projects collectively fish haus, and several interesting micro architecture projects emerged, one of which was developed by a large team led by Brigitta Kunsch. That project consisted of an aerodynamically shaped cabin, a 'hard tent', raised above the ground and used as a base for skiing weekends or short recreational surfing trips. The cabin was designed to be a tight fit, 'sitting only', short-stay home for two, with bed, mini-bar and sound system. It had to be transported on the roof of a car, so the weight limit was predetermined at 50kg. This meant that the construction had to be carbon fibre or aluminium. The student team made a detailed 1:20 model which included the support frame and crucially the interface between frame and shell. The reference we used to help the students with this design problem was a detail developed by Charles and Ray Eames for the connection between the thin steel frame support of their plywood chair. The frame shell interface is handled by a 45mm circular rubber washer that allows the frame to be lightly bolted to the plywood shell without causing cracking that would occur if there had been a rigid connection.

Frank Greenaway | Dorling Kindersley | Getty Images

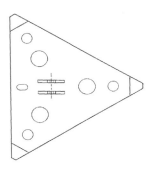
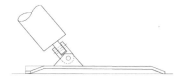
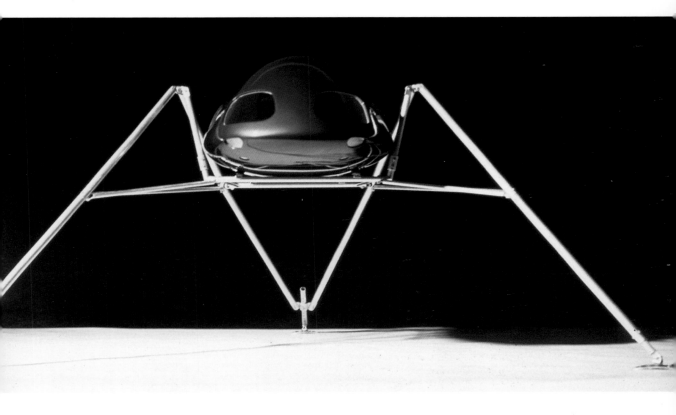

Project	Cabins, 2001	
Location	Mobile	
Students	Matthias Pektor	
	Christoph Roettinger	
Teaching Team	Prof. Richard Horden	
	Christian Kern	
	Lydia Haack	
Materials	Carbon Fibre, Aluminium,	
	Mylar Sails	

design team

carbon-fibre house

The project provides shelter for board sailing clubs with on-beach shelter for the storage and maintenance of boards. The whole kit can be delivered to beach sites trailed behind a car and assembled by a team of four board-sailors. The objective was to design a product that is attractive enough to win sponsorship from sailing companies and international organizations such as North Sails and Carbospars. The built project may then provide a platform for sponsors at race meetings in a similar way to the 'point lookout' and 'beach point' projects, exciting developments in a new field of 'sport architecture'. This project was informed by yacht and sail technology. The students developed and built their own mock-up of part of the frame which is essentially a composite lightweight structural panel comprising carbon-fibre sheet, foam infill and aluminium tubes. Roof and wall panels are velcro-connected Mylar sails with glass wishbone stiffeners.

full-size sample

design team

Project	Munich, 1997	**Teaching Team**	Prof. Richard Horden
Location	River Ammer, Saulgrub		Andreas Vogler
Students	Jean-Paul Amato	**Consultants**	Prof. Albert Pernpeitner
	Johannes Talhof		Prof. Stefan Winter
		Materials	Aluminium, HTP-plastic
		Dimensions	24.60 x 4.40 x 3.35m

kayak club

'Kayak club' is a mobile club house for canoeists. It was developed for a well-known kayak course on the River Ammer in the Bavarian Alps. The aluminium structure can also be used as a floating sales point or checkpoint during competitions. The unit construction system is transported in a dismantled state in a set of floating containers, which also serve as floats for the aluminium structure and as moorings for the kayaks. The 'kayak club' can therefore be transported to locations that are accessible only by kayak, where it can be fixed in position and erected within only a few hours. The connections are designed as simple hinged joints, which create a flexible structure capable of adapting to the movement of the water.

The structure was influenced by this Cessna seaplane.

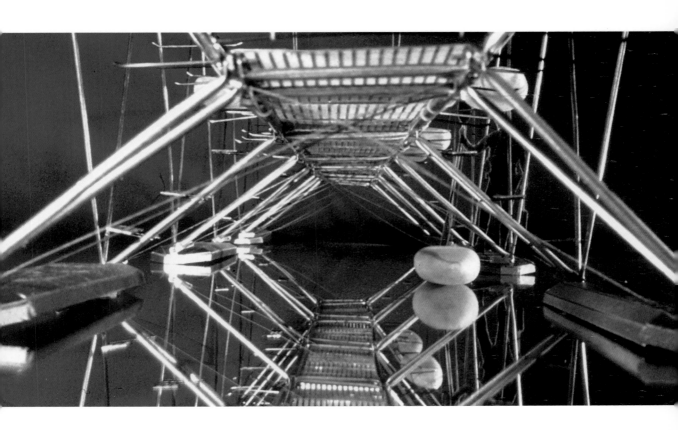

Project	Munich, 2003	**Teaching Team**	Prof. Richard Horden
Location	Loch Ness		Burkhard Franke
Students	Stoyan Todorov		

design team

loch ness

This project is undoubtedly conceived as jewelry for the landscape using this toroidal Mobius curve, much like a three-dimensional figure-of-eight. This elegant continuous, gently twisting, tubular form not only expresses something of the mythical creature of the loch but enters both land and water smoothly and lightly and without disturbing the delicate continuity of the shoreline. A museum may be conceived of as a sequence of spaces through which the visitor moves whilst experiencing the 'story' from entrance to exit. In this case the visitor enters and descends downwards to the introduction space and moves upwards to the view of the lake and then again down into the waters of the loch, with submarine 'windows' to view the 'creature' or life below the surface and finally rises upwards to the highest level where an elegant bar is located, offering a spectacular view over the loch, where visitors can celebrate the experience with a small glass of whisky.

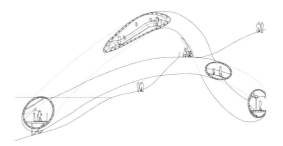

Project	Venice, 2003	**Teaching Team**	Prof. Richard Horden
Location	Laguna of Venice		Burkhard Franke
Students	Eva-Maria Hopper		Lydia Haack
	Sidonie Kade		

design team

serenissima

Naturally Venice is a favourite venue for our student projects. The city is only a 40-minute flight with Air Dolomiti across the Alps from Munich and five hours by train and approximately 7–8 hours drive along the east Riva coast of Lake Garda. The project brief was for a floating 'temporary island' summer school to be built on barges at Marghera. Each functioning part of the Summer School could be towed into position using light tugs and held in place in the lagoon with vertical steel and timber piles which are characteristic of the Venetian marine landscape. Students developed a charming solution using the mosaic street pattern of the Rialto region and contained it within a strict square footprint. This micro Venice had its own Grand Canal wide enough for single direction traffic of *sandolos*, gondolas and Riva launches and water taxis. The Serenissima Summer School project had a central urban square with cafés and a student restaurant with studios and residential colleges, each part separately constructed as a piece of the urban mosaic and containing its own energy systems and waste storage. The two students developed a diagonal structural system that echoed the vertical grain of Venetian architecture and created a fine lace-like appearance which wrapped both façade and roof.

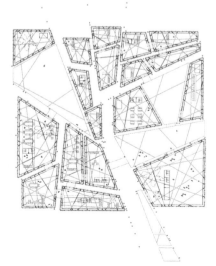

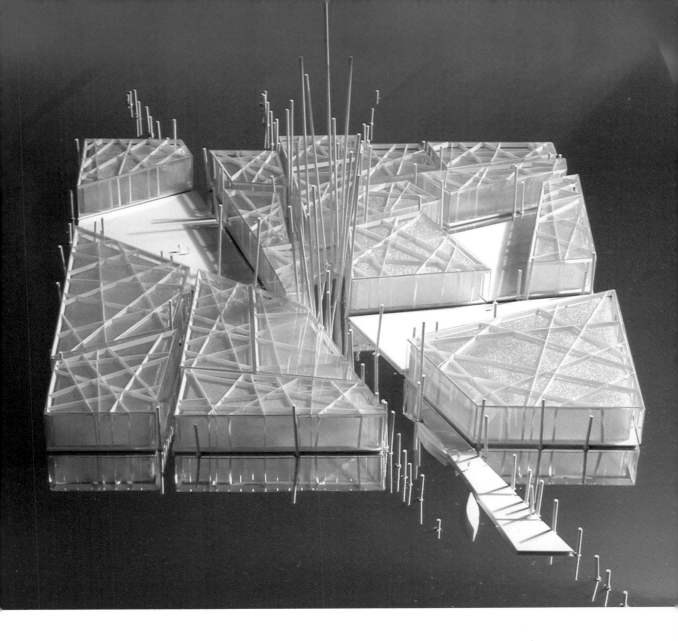

design team

Project	Venice, 2003	**Teaching Team**	Prof. Richard Horden
Location	Laguna of Venice		Christian Kern
Students	Hannah Schubert	**Consultants**	Francesca Depol,
	Alexander Remke		Consortio venetia nuova

summer art
school

The summer art school is located in the lagoon close to an island called San Lazzaro. There is a visual link to the Biennale area in Venice. An image of parked *sandolos* on land, which was taken by the students during the Venice field trip, was the guiding image for this sculptural design. The floating platforms on water are protected from rain and sun by three slightly sloped roof constructions which are open towards the bottom. The atelier spaces underneath are lit indirectly by the sun's reflections on the water.

GP

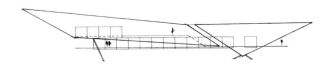

design team	Project	Munich, 2006/07	Teaching Team	Prof. Richard Horden
	Location	Lake Constance		Nadine Zinser
	Student	Florian Dressler	Consultants	Prof. Roy Fleetwood,
				VUW, New Zealand

'iPod'™ house

We had first studied the idea of compact, sitting-only spaces in the Minox Camera House in 2000. The idea was to slim the form of a house down to its absolute minimum, a space similar in height to the fuselage of a Lear Jet or Cessna Citation, that is, around 1.7m. It was essential to have standing spaces in the design, not only for movement but also for dressing, cooking and showering. The sitting-only spaces could then be arranged off the central circulation route. A key advantage of the design is that all component parts of this factory-produced home are small and light enough to be shipped inside a standard ISO freight container. We borrowed the name of the Apple product 'iPod'™ as a working concept to emphasize the sleek character of the home and its highly efficient function. The project formed a part of our programme for a European Concept House and went on to inform the 'solar pebble' project (page 260), the 'family compact home' projects (pages 254–58) in 2008 and the 'New Zealand out-bach' (page 198).

LUFTHANSA | APPLE

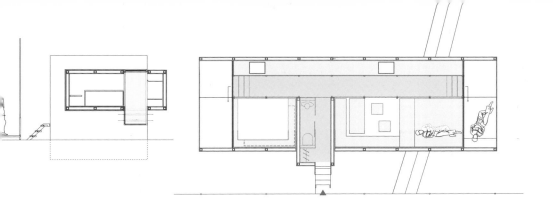

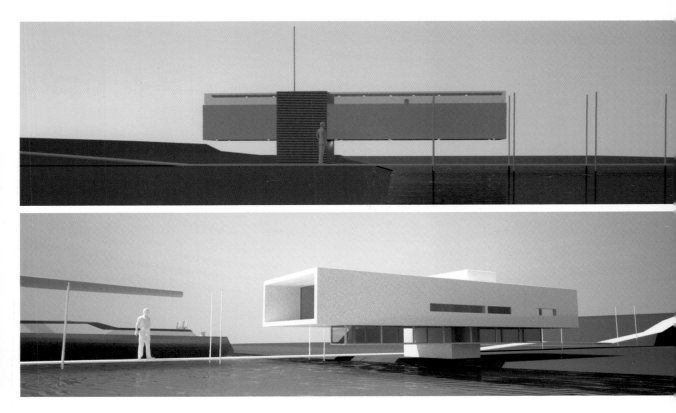

Outside my home on Poole Harbour the seabirds balance effortlessly on the up-draught at Evening Hill. Suddenly they dive down under the water to catch a fish and then rise into the air vertically, without rotors or high octane aviation fuel, shedding the heavy seawater whilst carrying their fresh new 0.4-kilo meal – no human vehicle can achieve this! Nature is extraordinarily advanced and presents us, I believe, with high efficiency, low energy, low technology answers and not only to flight and marine innovations but to every field of life, if we choose to learn.

The duck of course uses its feet to paddle, dive, swim under water, walk, and provide initial thrust for take off. If a duck had a propellor it would get hopelessly tangled up in one of its essential food sources, weed! The duck also achieves a relatively fast speed with high efficiency and very little disturbance to the water surface. The backwards looking splashing action of a rowing boat looks quite crude by comparison. The issue it seemed was could we learn something that might help to progress low energy boat propulsion?

cc/OO11 TU_Fin | solar proa

Playstation Too (Adria 38) at Villa D'Este, Lake Como, Italy

RH

design team	**Project**	Munich
	Location	Lakes around Munich
	Team	Prof. Richard Horden,
		Tim Wessbecher
	Consultants	Martin Francis, Gilberto
		Penzo

RH

cc/001

Martin Francis, the yacht designer, and Gilberto Penzo from Venice, a boat expert and author of *The Gondola*, advised our student teams on the initial stages of carbon hull design. The challenge we threw to our students was to drive their boats up the Grand Canal in Venice. 'TU-FiN' (see page 174) is now ready to achieve that!

I often work in parallel with my students on a slightly different design to help to speed and inform the design process and to enable a lateral look at the problems. This is both intellectually challenging and can help both students and Institute to achieve a progressive design. In this case I worked in parallel with the 'TU-FiN' group on an alternative 'duck drive' system.

This manual drive boat 'cc/001' (canard concept/001) was inspired in part by 'Playstation Too' sailing on Lake Como off the Hotel Villa d'Este, (see page 171). I admired the beautiful carbon hull shape and straight bow and saw the need for a slim, light, elegant personal boat for hotels, which could carry two or four and be hand driven for fitness whilst facing forward. The gondolier drives a 500kg boat with six tourists on board, also weighing in at 500kgs. So he moves a weight of one ton at four knots, with one oar, whilst singing and of course looking ahead! The oars for 'cc/001' must not protrude sideways because of manoeuvring in tight spaces in marinas etc., which meant looking into a human version of the duck's feet. This is far more complex than may first appear, the duck's feet rotate around 180 degrees from front to rear. There are many options to be tested and first attempts proved high manoeuvrability but very poor boat speed.

The issue is still intensely interesting and we will build this elegant hull shape at full scale in carbon with alternative rigs for testing human and solar energy propulsion and later with assisted fluidic muscle technology.

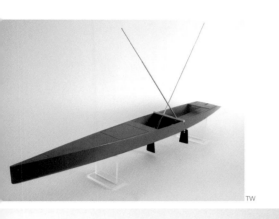

TU_FiN
Walking on Water

TU_FIN

'TU_FiN' was developed with the thought of bringing environmental awareness to a sport, leisure, and fitness boat. The innovative fin drive corresponds to nature's example (duck feet) and guarantees maximum speed without any noise pollution. The driver operates the boat while facing forward in an upright position. The elliptical course of movement is equivalent to the one performed on a cross-trainer device found in many gyms. It activates nearly all muscles without harming any joints and so ensures an integral, invigorating cardiovascular workout. After completing the project at the TU Munich and exhibiting at the trade fair in Düsseldorf 'Boot 07' in January, the student team privately financed the calculation and building of a prototype, which is now in testing and being further developed to go into serial production. 'TU_FiN' has been awarded the Pininfarina Design Prize for Transportation Design in 2007.

design team	Project	Munich	Teaching Team	Prof. Richard Horden
	Location	Lakes around Munich		Nadine Zinser
	Students	Ballmeier, Dreßler,	Consultants	Martin Francis,
		Eichelberg, Kiryakov		Gilberto Penzo
			Sponsors	UnternehmerTUM,
				Private Project
			Materials	Carbon fibre, epoxy,
				Nomex-Honeycomb
			Dimensions	length: 6m, width: 1.2m
			Weight	approx. 60kg

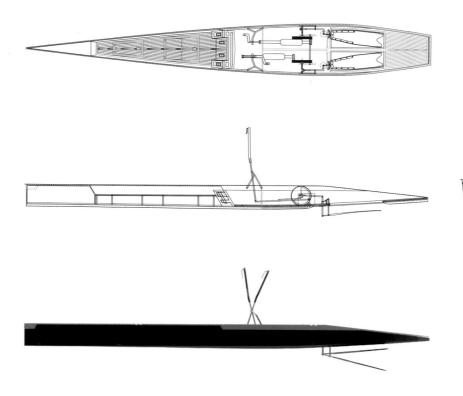

Project	Munich, 2006	**Teaching Team**	Prof. Richard Horden
Location	Mobile		Wieland Schmidt
Students	Andreas Schwab	**Consultants**	Martin Francis, boat
	Tibor Bartholomä		designer, London
	Daniel Boos		Gilberto Penzo, boat builder,
	Carolin Dißmann		Venice

design team

solar proa

The solar power boat is a concept boat for the average family. It has space for six people including the driver, multifunctional, innovative technology and materials and can be operated without a driver's license. It is also light and elegant. These are all fundamental issues that were considered during the development and design process. Our final product, the 'proa', is an asymmetric catamaran that is completely powered by solar energy and made from carbon fibre. The dynamic, asymmetric shape allows for a large surface of 14.5m for the solar panels. To avoid a drift towards starboard, it works with a similar principle as the gondolas in Venice – it has a longer waterline on the side towards the small hull. A symmetric, streamline shape underneath the waterline reduces the drag to a minimum. Above the waterline the shape is dominated by edges that set a new standard for innovative and modern boat design.

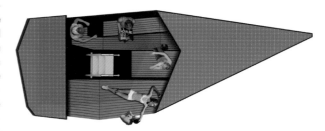

As children at school in the English beech and pine wood countryside, we made many early experiments with houses tunnelled into the hard sandy ground and within the tree canopies. The instinct to build is in all of us to varying degrees and the tree house may seem a topic to discard with childhood but we embrace the opportunity in our micro architecture studies at the TU Munich. Young hopeful entrants to the Architecture Faculty are asked to draw a bicycle or a tree house and one of the reasons we do this is to see if the aspiring student has a grasp of triangulation and of course to check drawing technique. As with all of our micro architecture projects the design of a contemporary timber, aluminium or carbon tree house requires a knowledge of material and weight, triangulation, potential for product design, for prefabrication and stability with minimum disturbance to the natural landscape. If the projects are built it is required that they be approved by our University engineering department, so students have an additional lesson in negotiating the German DIN standards procedure.

landscape

folding canopies | tree tent | air camp | one kilo house | geodetic balloons | camera house | spiral lab|
| New Zealand out-bach | cocoon |

The Gibbs Farm Sculpture Park, Kaipara, North Island, New Zealand   RH

design team		
Project	RHA London, 1994	
Location	Buckingham Palace	
Team	Mira Esposito	
	Sarah Forbes Waller	
	Richard Horden	
	Brian Kelly	
	Billie Lee	
	Sarah North	
Consultants	Tony Hunt	
	Clyde Malby	

folding canopies

In early 1994 our office in London was invited to design an elegant shelter for visitors to the courtyards and grounds of Buckingham Palace during the Summer Opening. The gently unfolding 'umbrellas' evolved naturally from this title and were further inspired by the image of Italian market canopies. The idea was to provide the palace with a light, adaptable custom-designed series of canopies, which could be used throughout the year for garden parties and outdoor concerts, as well as for the Summer Opening. The canopies were designed on a 12-ft module which echoed the one used by John Nash in the design of Buckingham Palace early in the nineteenth century, and set up a relationship between the canopies and the Palace architecture. The project was unfortunately abandoned by Buckingham Palace officials before it was seen by members of the Royal Family and the design is awaiting further development.

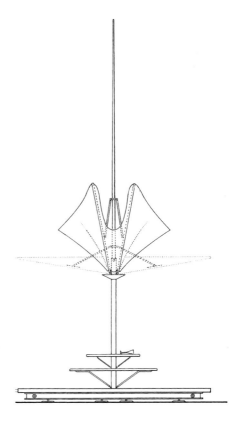

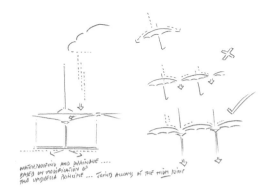

WATERPROOFING AND DRAINAGE ....
BASED ON MODIFICATION OF
THE UMBRELLA PRINCIPLE ... JOINTS ALWAYS AT THE HIGH POINT

Prototype in the grounds of Windsor Castle

RH

folding canopies | 183

Project	Tree Tent, 2002–03	**Teaching Team** Prof. Richard Horden
Location	Forest (mobile)	Claudia Pöppel
Students	Ralf Drewing	
	Petra Liedl	
	Richard Schindler	
	Markus Vogl	

design team

tree tent

This topic has always generated great energy at our micro architecture classes at the TU Munich. We start with a briefing for a tree house that can be light enough to be carried into a forest and unfolded and lifted into the tree using a rope over a branch without damage to flora or fauna. The target weight limit is normally set to whatever can be carried by one or two people, around 26kg maximum. Our optimum solution to date is the 'tree-brella'. This is a large inverted, 2.6m-diameter, umbrella that can be hoisted, point upwards, into the tree while folded tightly to avoid damage to, or snagging on, branches. When the 'tree-brella' reaches it's height limit close to the host branch, the rope, which trails from the lower umbrella 'handle', can be pulled to open up the canopy above and the textile floor below. Two full-size tree-brellas have been built by our teams and the idea has expanded in recent studies to larger, 6m-diameter versions for giant tree-canopy exploration in remote regions.

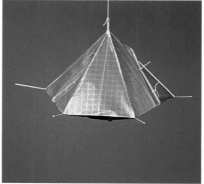

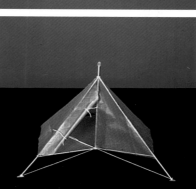

Project	Munich, 1998	**Sponsoring**	Krah Seilsicherungen,
Location	National Park		Garmisch-Partenkirchen
	Bavarian Forest		Vilsmayer Metallbau,
Students	Julia Haas		Pfarrkofen
	Andreas Kienle		W. Junge Sportartikelmarket-
Teaching Team	Prof. Richard Horden		ing, Witten
	Eva Neumeyer		MTH Zeltbau, Schechingen
	Andreas Vogler		Ploch Segelmacherei, Munich
Consultant	Vilsmayer Metallbau,	**Materials**	Aluminium, Rip-stop Nylon
	Pfarrkofen	**Dimensions**	1.8 x 1.8 x 1.4m
		Weight	15kg

design team

air camp

'Air camp' was designed as an observation point for a wildlife sanctuary in the Bavarian Forest. This modern tree house provides protection from animals in the park and can be used as a platform for wildlife photographers or for campers. In its dismantled state, 'air camp' can be carried in a rucksack by a single person and assembled with a minimum of effort. The platform consists of a square frame of aluminium tubes, between which a fabric base is spanned. It is braced by a three-dimensional structure of aluminium rods that also form a supporting framework for the tent skin. Details and materials are based on high-tech developments in mountaineering equipment and hang-gliders. 'Air camp' was presented to a broader public at the 'European outdoor fair 98' in Friedrichshafen and at the 'Caravan Salon 98' in Düsseldorf.

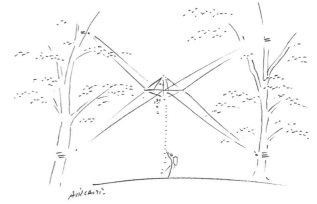

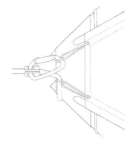

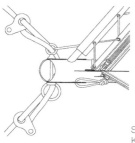

Student Andreas Kienle high up in the tree tops.

design team

Project Munich, 2001
Location Munich (mobile)
Students Tillmann Kühnel
Moritz Mungenast
Klaus Puchta

Teaching Team Prof. Richard Horden
Thomas Straub

one kilo house

The aim of our project was to design an emergency shelter for one person with some baggage. It should offer protection against extreme weather, a basic possibility of retreat and a sleeping place. It could function as a dignified location for homeless people or for people who need to live in a city temporarily without a fixed residence of their own. We developed a modular system consisting of an aluminium-rod construction with a fixed floor panel and a tent that can be attached to it. Depending on demand, the framework might be installed by the city or by a private organization for a longer period of time. Sanitary and technical care would be provided by public facilities located nearby. The design offers possibilities for other uses, such as playground shelters for children or as a platform for people enjoying the sun. During the day the tent can be folded into a triangular backpack containing a person's essential, individual property. In the evening it can be easily set up again by connecting it to the tube structure by small hooks.

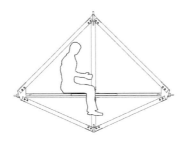

design team	**Project**	Aberdeen, 1986 Moscow, 1991	**Consultants**	Kathy Horden Richard Horden Tony Hunt Robin Webster Florian Fischötter
			Material	Melinex
			Dimensions	6m diameter
			Weight	100gms

geodetic balloons

Both Moscow and Aberdeen are located close to latitude 57°, so in both these areas with the cold air temperature we were able to achieve elegant, light-weight, floating geodetic structures. These are basically triangulated balloons made from metal-coated foil and joined using adhesive tape. The balloons are filled with heated air. The purpose was to teach students geodetic construction and the importance of achieving more structure with less material. There was also the aspect of 'fun and function'. With a lot of energy and enthusiasm students in Aberdeen built model pro-totypes and drove to remote snowy hillsides to launch their architecture into bright, crystal-blue skies. In Moscow, students powered their balloons and spirits with vodka. A first vodka-powered flight!

RH

RH

Project	Munich, 2001	**Teaching Team**	Prof. Richard Horden
Location	Riegsee, Garmisch		Thomas Straub
Students	Kerstin Engelhardt	**Materials**	Aluminium, Double Glazing
	Torsten Schlauersbach		

design team

camera house

The students took their inspiration for the project from the famous Minox 8 x 11mm 'spy' camera. The aim was to achieve high-quality living in a small area with a compact, technologically advanced design. This micro architecture house was also meant to function as a portable nature 'hide', capable of being installed by boat or inflatable floats amongst a reed-edged lake or river. Such conditions exist in the Pre-Alps south of Munich. In this case the students chose their own specific location at the Riegsee to make the relationship between architecture and nature as realistic as possible. The insulating outer aluminium shells can slide apart, revealing the fully glazed enclosure that offers a great view of the surrounding nature.

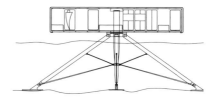

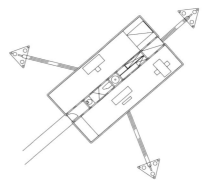

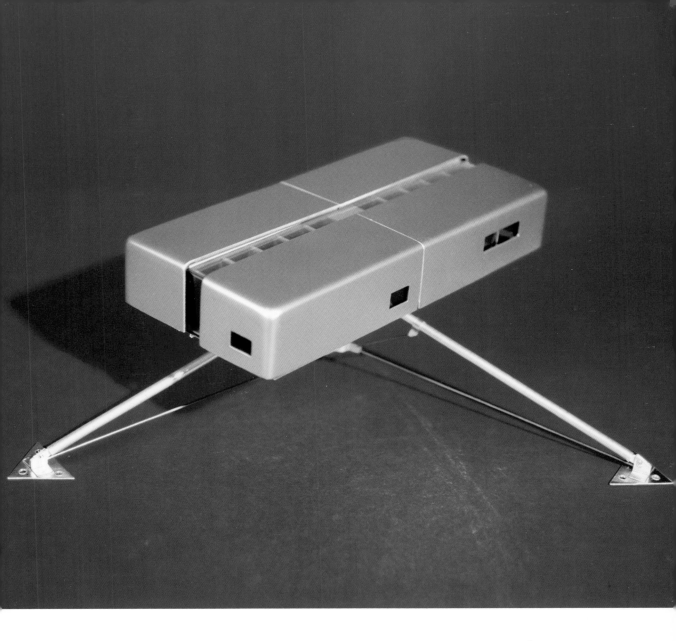

spiral lab

The Study Gallery of Modern Art in Poole tries to extend the common understanding of the museum by bringing together artists and art enthusiasts to exchange experiences, study together and to actually produce art. The design task was to create a mobile unit that enables the gallery to extend this programme outside Poole and which serves as a field base and space for all kinds of events and workshops. It was especially important to translate the light, open character of the gallery to its smaller satellite without copying the architecture. The spiral shape frame structure which is significant for the design of 'art lab' identifies it as an art object in itself. The final building may be realized with the generous support of Jem Main, director of The Study Gallery in Poole. Five frames were installed in the sculpture courtyard of The Study Gallery in spring 2005.

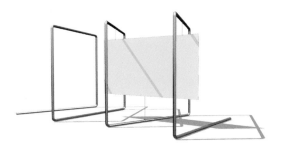

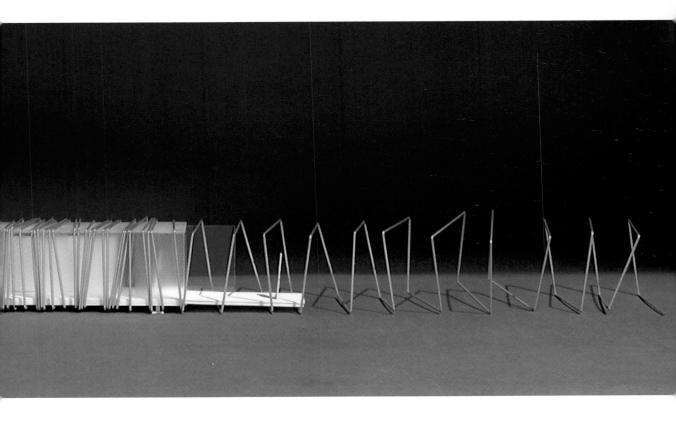

design team

Project
Location

Students

Munich, 2004
Courtyard of The Study
Gallery, Poole

Caroline Haberkorn
Christine Schmidt

Teaching Team

Consultant

Sponsoring

Prof. Richard Horden
Burkhard Franke
Tim Wessbecher

Jem Main, director of
The Study Gallery, Poole
Marijke de Goey, artist

Jem Main, The Study Gallery
Werner Olschok, Fa. Rösch
Fa. Hülsen, Rohrbogen
Klöckner Stahl- und Met-
allhandel, Metallwerkstatt
Lingenfelder

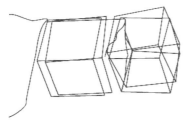

Bracelet by
Marijke de Goey

Colour sample

Prototype of the
rotating joint
connection

The Study Gallery of
Modern Art, Poole

Project	Munich, 2006	**Teaching Team**	Prof. Richard Horden
Location	New Zealand		Burkhard Franke
Students	Tristan Franke		Wieland Schmidt
	Daniel Haimerl		Nadine Zinser
	Valton Limani	**Consultant**	Prof. Albert Pernpeitner
	Simone Mans		Prof. Roy Fleedwood,
	Tina Rau		University of Wellington
	Julia Wolf		

design team

New Zealand out-bach

'Bach' is the name for a New Zealand weekend beach or hillside home. The primary aim is to live outside but with shelter from heavy winds and rain storms when required. The project shows a rigorous programme for a linear deck-like structure that could be located on the water's edge or on a sloping wooded landfall. Small rectangular units are bolted to the pier/deck on either side to provide the necessary but minimal seated-only height, as well as sleeping, cooking or living accommodation. The proposed pier/deck may have an added glass or textile roof covering but generally would remain open sided. Our students worked to International ISO standard container dimensions so that the whole out-bach could be built in Europe and shipped to the waterside in New Zealand. The design owes a lot to the flush deck architecture of the highly styled Italian 'Wally Yacht'. All systems concealed in hatches and ropes disappear through stainless-steel slotted fair leads to highly powered winches below deck.

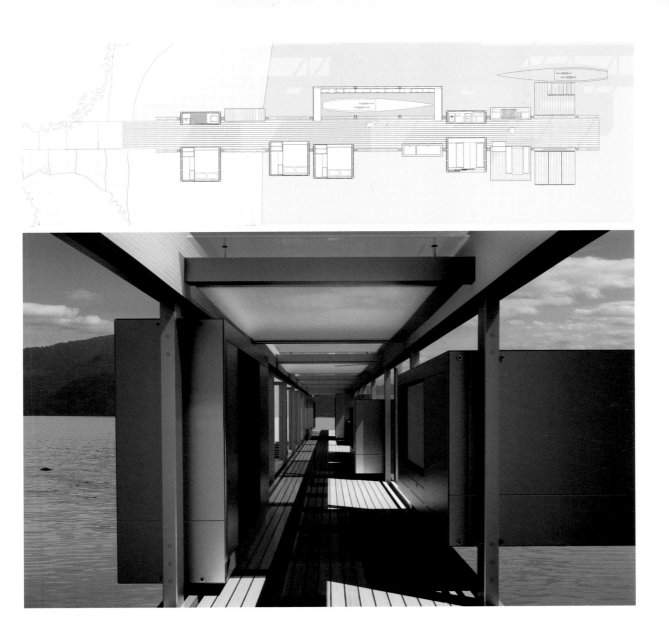

design team

Project	Munich, 2007	**Teaching Team**	Prof. Richard Horden
Location	Kauri coast,		Burkhard Franke
	New Zealand		
Students	Andreas Schwab		
	Marius Timermann		

cocoon

The 'cocoon' is a temporary accommodation for backpackers travelling through New Zealand. It is intended to be located on the Kauri coast on the North Island. Kauri trees are among the tallest in the world, reaching heights of more than 50 metres. The task was to design an economic building that was sympathetic to the natural environment and required a minimum amount of grey energy. The inspiration for the form was the nest of a spider that has a unique shape, a light, lucent structure, which offers protection and is perfectly adapted for hanging in trees. Carbon-fibre tubes form seven asymmetric crosses that are twisted at an angle of 45 degrees towards each other. The construction is covered using ropes and a membrane to form a lightweight structure that can be hung from a tree without damaging the trunk or branches.

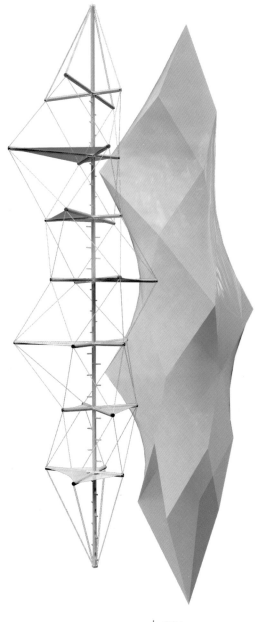

The penguin chick has long been a guide and reference for our projects for the Antarctic from the design of the 'm-igloo' in 2003 to a recent project for a large ice station to accommodate 24 scientists and explorers. The penguin chick has developed over five million years to its curving, compact pyramid-like form which is ideal for resisting high wind forces and for conserving energy in a similar way to a Swiss thermos flask: a small, minimally exposed head and round body with the centre of gravity sitting as low as possible. Of course it also uses two feet and its tail for balance and stability, a three-point support structure similar to that in most of our micro-architecture projects. The fine feathers also help to conserve heat. The soft, fluffy penguin chick is a land bird much lower in height and not designed for swimming like its taller and more mobile and fluid dynamic parents, so its features are uniquely applicable to our attempts to create stable, efficient shelter in this challenging region.

Chinstrap penguin (Pygoscelis antarctica) on iceberg, summer

polar regions

m-igloo | polar lab | ice station | point penguin | tripolar | rts

design team

Project	Munich, 2002–03	**Teaching Team**	Prof. Richard Horden Lydia Haack
Location	Antarctic (mobile)	**Consultant**	A. Pernpeintner, TUM
Students	Ilona Gallitzdörfer Christine Müller		

m-igloo

One of the main goals with this design was the minimization of size, so that the unit could be transported by helicopter or in a standard shipping container. However, it still has to offer enough space for two people to survive and to spend a few days in it in a region of extreme cold. This required an extremely effective insulated skin, and a shape with optimal wind resistance. The basic form and structure were taken from the Ski-Doo™ snowmobile, but also from the tobogganing penguin! They have inhabited Antarctica for millions of years, while man has only been visiting for the last 100 or so, and not very comfortably!

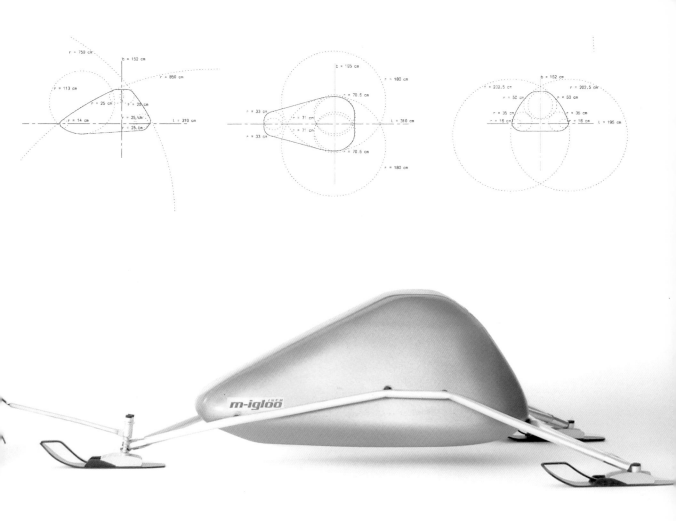

polar lab

'Polar lab' is a temporary Antarctic habitat and research station deployable by helicopter or standard transportation sledges. The basic idea was to design an independently functioning capsule that could be delivered in one drop, and was capable of housing three people for a period of up to three weeks without need for further supplies. 'Polar lab' combines a simple structure and an optimal volume–surface ratio for aerodynamics, energy-efficiency, simple construction and potential for serial fabrication. At the same time 'polar lab' is capable of expanding its volume to create optimal research conditions. This is achieved by using the simple geometric form of a regular octahedron which can be expanded with three additional tetrahedrons. The habitat must have relatively small windows as in summer months in the Antarctic the sun never sets and has a low altitude.

Project	Munich, 2006	**Teaching Team** Prof. Richard Horden
Location	Antarctic (mobile)	Wieland Schmidt
Students	Simone Hiesinger	
	Michael Kehr	
	Eike Schling	
	Sandra Spindler	

design team

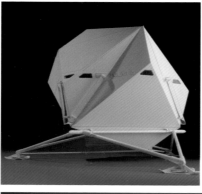
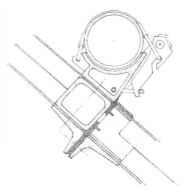
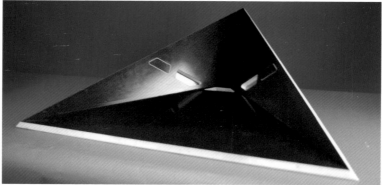

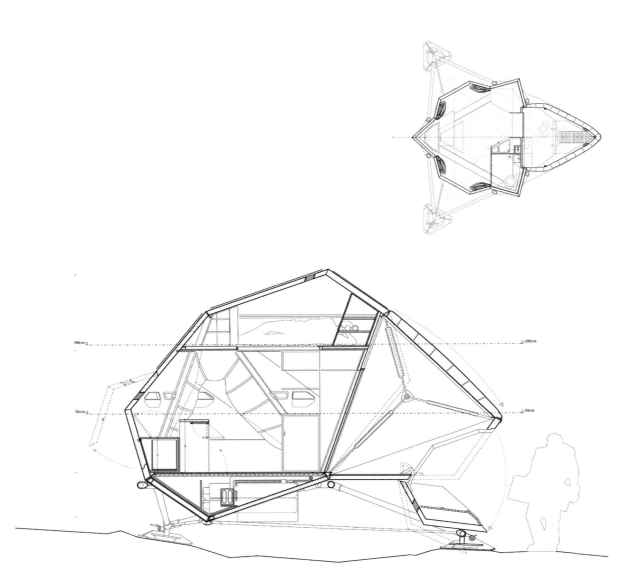

design team	**Project**	Munich, 2006	**Teaching Team**	Prof. Richard Horden
	Location	Antarctic (mobile)		Wieland Schmidt
	Students	Simone Hiesinger		
		Sandra Spindler		

ice station

Transportation and delivery of the 'ice station' to varying locations in this extreme environment is the first challenge for the designers of Antarctic habitats. This project uses a helicopter delivery of between 0.7 to 1.3 tons for the five elements of the construction: three-point adjustable base frame, a two-level central social space, and the three double-deck sleeping and working compartments, which provide space for up to six explorers or scientists. The structure requires a tough multi-layer thermal outer jacket to prevent ice forming in the tight gaps between the separate units. This was one of our first projects to use the penguin chick as a starting point, an ideal form for thermal efficiency. The wide base provides stability in high wind, while the narrow top minimizes heat loss from the top. The station entrance on the ground is in a down-wind position, and the downward curved shape of the underside encourages wind scouring of the snow at the base which maintains a hollow around the perimeter and aids access.

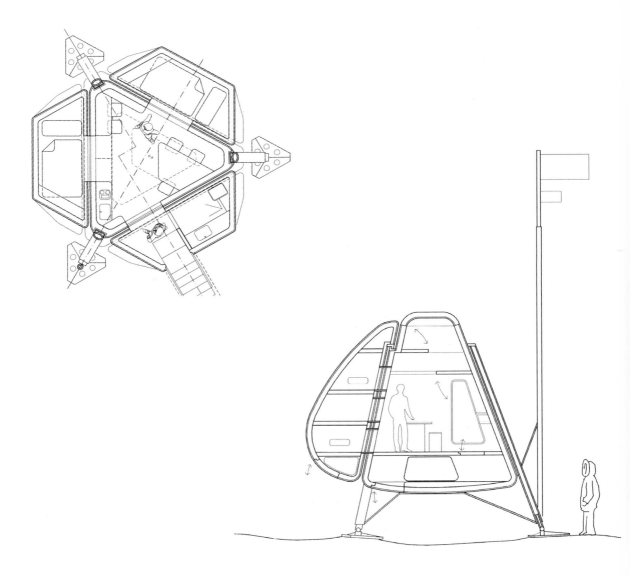

point penguin

Construction in the Antarctic is often interrupted by sudden weather changes and high winds. This design allows the three-legged pyramid frame to be built first and the soft, composite outer skins added next. Then, the prefabricated interior cabins and social spaces can be installed in a protected environment, and construction carried on for 24-hour periods if required. The joined units create a central atrium area that contains social spaces and open circulation by way of stairs or ramps. This arrangement gets away from the usually cramped conditions of the more traditional human Antarctic habitat which involves living along a corridor. The top of 'point penguin' houses an observation area with a radio station and bar for viewing the stars and aurora and for communications. The larger, lower area at the base contains food, water and drinks storage adding mass for stability. Two 'point penguin' habitation units provide living and social facilities for 52 scientists, explorers or guides and visitors.

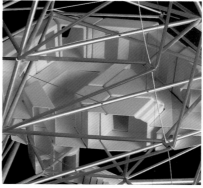

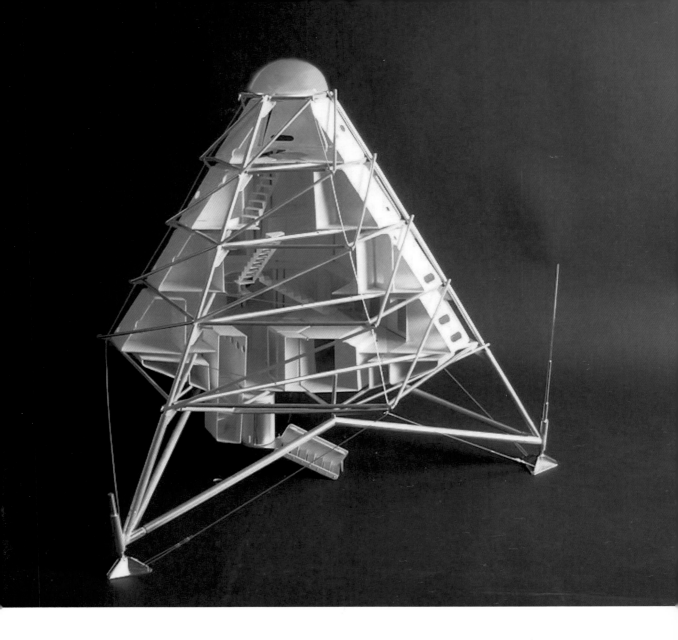

Project	Munich, 2006	**Teaching Team**	Prof. Richard Horden
Location	Antarctic (mobile)		Wieland Schmidt
Student	Juae Kim		Walter Klasz
		Consultant	Guido Kleffel, AWI

design team

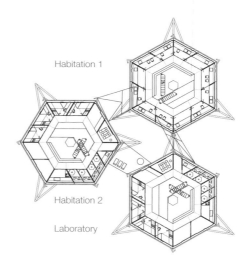

Habitation 1

Habitation 2

Laboratory

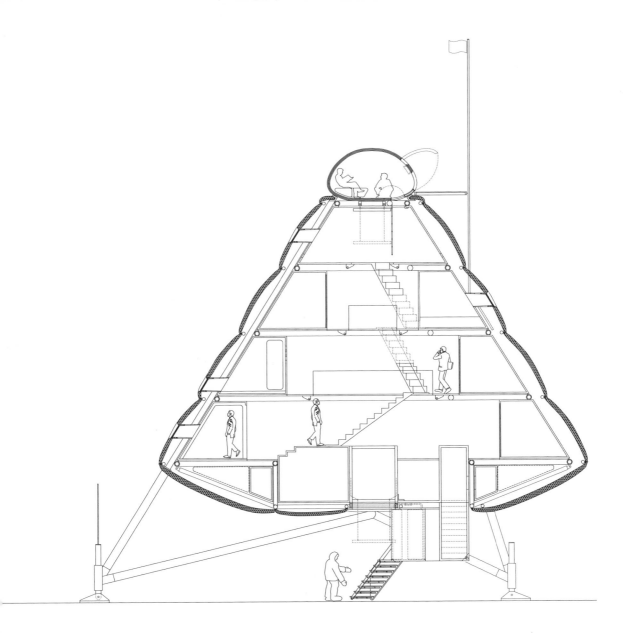

design team		
Project	Munich, 2005	**Teaching Team** Prof. Richard Horden
Location	Antarctic (mobile)	Wieland Schmidt
Students	Simon Vorhammer	**Consultant** Guido Kleffel, AWI
	Robin Renner	

tripolar

'Tripolar' is a design for a permanent modern research station in the Antarctic that will provide work and living facilities for more than 20 people. The compact, energy-efficient and aerodynamic form is designed with an inner core which can be built using elemental construction methods, and a modular outer rim, thus saving space during shipping and in the cost of transport. The exterior is covered in a triangulated grid of insulated sandwich panels. The two-level core includes all the 'public' facilities, such as an illuminated workspace and bathrooms on the upper floor and further bathrooms, bar, kitchen, and a living room on the ground floor. The outer module loop contains the private habitations for the researchers. Separated laboratories are conceived in a linear extendable system.

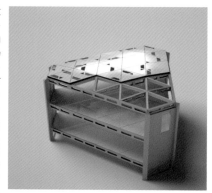

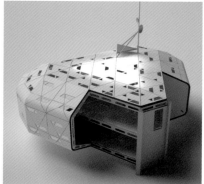

It is built in four steps: set up the frame, add built-in floorplates, set up of the roof, fit the modular cladding.

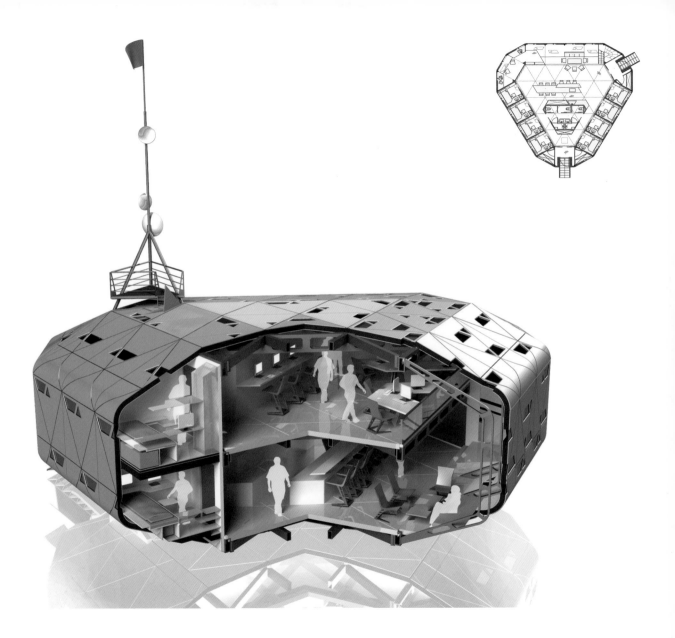

design team		
Project	Munich, 2007	**Teaching Team** Prof. Richard Horden
Location	Potter Cove,	Nadine Zinser
	King George Island,	**Consultant** Guido Kleffel, AWI
	Antarctic	Prof. Albert Pernpeitner
Students	Peter Holzner	
	Florian Brummann	

rts

The 'rts' (research-technology-shelter) consists of optimized and pre-installed modules. Part of an adaptable programme, they can be transported in 20m-high cube containers and installed in all weather in a split-level arrangement. This assembled structure allows for a central supply channel and good illumination and can be changed or expanded easily. The aerodynamic form is optimized by elevating of the bases. The living station for 20 people is separated into a quiet private zone and common spaces made up of several modules. The strict standardization of the modules helps compensate for the costs of sophisticated materials.

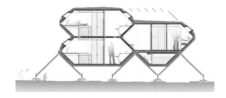

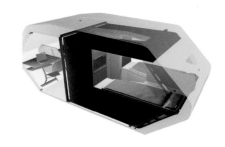

Deserts vary widely in climatic and geological character so we study the flora, fauna and special climate within the chosen desert area to gain a greater understanding of the way nature inhabits these special extreme locations. We then explore the positive influences that these may have on the design of human habitats. We have students and teaching assistants who have special experience of these regions, as was the case with a recent student from South Africa. Her personal knowledge of the Namibian Desert brought special insight to the conditions of this region on the South West Atlantic Coast of Africa and informed the design of the Lizard Lodge in a unique way.

desert flight | desert lodge

Dunes between Timbuktu and Taoudeni, Mali

WS

deserts

Project Munich, 2007
Location Namibian Desert
Students Matthäus Deffner
Christian Heck
Teaching Team Prof. Richard Horden
Lydia Haack

Consultants Dr. ing. A. Pernpeintner,
Dept. for Aerodynamic,
TUM

design team

desert flight

The project is essentially a very light tent built within the aluminium framework of an enlarged hang-glider. When the glider is in the nose-down, resting position and facing into the wind, the white wings form a shield, which in this design protects the black inner tent from sandstorms and direct sunlight. The inhabitants awake and prepare for the day's flight in the cool early morning air. To send the glider into flight, one end of a chord is attached to the centre of the hang-glider frame (much like a kite) and the other end tied to a camel-saddle frame. A camel team can travel at 30 kilometres an hour, providing sufficient power to lift a light hang-glider to 50 metres altitude from where, in the rising air thermals of the desert, the pilot of the hang-glider can drop the towing chord and begin rotations. The camel team and pilot can communicate by means of GPS, which allows them to coordinate and move on to the next desired landing and campsite location.

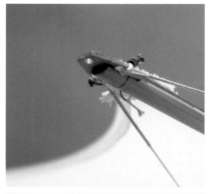

Project	Munich, 2007	
Location	African Steppe	
Students	Karin Wouters	
	Na Shen	
Teaching Team	Prof. Richard Horden	
	Burkhard Franke	

design team

desert lodge

Building on lessons learned from the natural inspiration for 'point penguin', this team made a thorough search of natural desert forms at the beginning of their research. One form that particularly caught their interest was the desert lizard which adopts a fascinating position when exposed to the hot desert environment.

The animal faces away from the sun with its mouth open. While its back is at a 45-degree angle to the sun, its chin and soft stomach tissue are shaded. The lizard also lifts each foot in turn to bring relief from the hot desert sand. The form is an interesting one for the the micro architecture team as it suggests a natural convection/thermal cooling movement from the lower back to the top of the head and naturally photovoltaic cells on the upward sloping back.

The project is conceived as a spine and legs of steel or aluminium to support an arrangement of prefabricated habitation modules that form the main body of the structure. The ground below the underside offers a shaded place for an oasis-like area that feature cacti and palm and perhaps a small pool. The solar cells on the back are spaced away from the habitation.

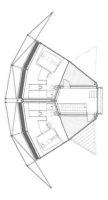

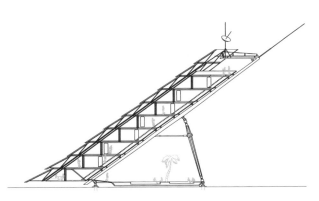

The designs of aviation and auto interiors have given us a knowledge of how to create high quality spaces in compact 'sitting only' situations.

Much of our work at the Institute is in analysing the potential for finding a healthy mix of sitting and standing spaces for a home. Traditional fishermen's cottages on the North Sea at Pennen in Scotland have beds like bunks in cupboards formed in the side of the rock cliff face. Today aircrew on long-haul flights use bunk beds within sophisticated modified airfreight containers as do submariners and crews of aircraft carriers.

We are used to spending a lot of time in our automobiles and on long-haul flights and in other micro environments. As work and leisure time increase we spend less time in our homes, which could be greatly reduced in size. Small modular homes can be factory produced and have recycling potential. They also offer the chance to reduce the embodied energy in the construction of the home as well as the energy consumed during use. There are also benefits in reducing the impact of the home on nature and increasing oxygen-giving green space and enhancing the pleasure of living with nature.

'less material more nature'

compact homes

River Mattig, Uttendorf, Austria

SK

design team

Project	Munich, 1992
Location	Europe
Students	Thomas Höger
	Oliver Stirling
	Michael Wigginton
Teaching Team	Prof. Richard Horden
	Sarah Kirby
Materials	Aluminium

skydeck house 1992

These projects began in 1972 with the 'yacht house', New Forest, England and then in 1992 with the 'skydeck house' project London, a project first designed in our office with Ove Arup and Partners and Jordan Engineering who had produced the bathrooms for the Lloyd's building. It is essentially a steel-framed, timber construction, 2.6m, modular terraced house. This can have units, like the skydeck roof barbecue point, delivered completely fitted out with furniture similar to the cockpit of a yacht and installed by crane after construction. It can then be extended up to five or seven storeys in height depending on the detailed construction method used.

KK

Project	Munich, 2000
Location	Europe
Students	Manuel Pittino
	Stefan Scholz
Teaching Team	Omar Guebel
	Prof. Richard Horden
Materials	Aluminium
Dimensions	2.6 x 2.6m Module

design team

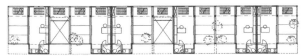

'Smart™ car' house

The Smart™ car has been a source of inspiration for our teams since its introduction by Mercedes in 1998. This project by two students at our institute was to design a compact home above a Smart™ car, integrating habitation and transportation. The Smart™ car dimensions are 2.69m long by 1.56m wide and 1.53m high. The basic habitation space in the 'Smart™ house' is provided in a cube of 2.6m and the hygiene facilities and entrance and stair are added in modules of 1.3 x 2.6m. This enables units to be stacked and accessed freely without disturbance to the occupants of lower cubes.

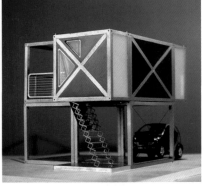

<table>
<tr><td>design team</td><td>**Project**
Location
Team</td><td>HCLA, London, 2002
London
Stefano Angaroni
Stephen Cherry
Adrian Fowler
Davis Franklin
Billie Lee
Peter Ludwig
Kwamina Monney
Jurgan Schubert
Andreas Vogler
Danielle Williams</td><td>**Team**

Consultants</td><td>Peter Zimmer
Prof. Richard Horden
Oscar Faber
HL Technik
MACE Ltd.
East London University
AYH Partnership
Freud Lemos Ltd.
Dalton Warner Davies</td></tr>
</table>

city arcade

This design with Stephen Cherry at our London office explored the benefits and potential for an urban arcade lifestyle. The light, arcaded architecture is inspired by the Eames House in California with eucalyptus trees lining the arcade and with a partial glass roof to temper the space. Electric-powered Smart™ cars are integrated into the design in a lift system at the ends of the glazed internal street. The cars can be called from the apartments and appear washed and dried and ready for use. Other ideas for reducing carbon emissions are also integral to the design.

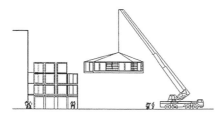

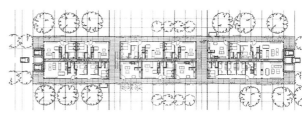

EO

Project	Munich, 2002–05	**Teaching Team**	Prof. Richard Horden
Location	Europe		Burkhard Franke
Students	V. Blacker-Sturm,		Lydia Haack
	V. Gruber,		Hendrik Müller
	C. Hainzlmeier,		Andreas Vogler
	S. Koch, B. Matern,		Tim Wessbecher
	D. Oswald, M. Penev,		Walter Klasz
	T. Tuhkanen		

design team

Concept and development: TU Munich, Institute Prof. Richard Horden

European and USA patents: Richard Horden

micro compact home [m-ch]

Elements of modern aircraft interiors have advanced our awareness of quality in compact personal spaces: indirect lighting and directed ventilation, integrated flat-screen displays, internet and mobile phone connectivity from 30,000 feet, carefully designed and scaled lightweight crockery and cutlery and, from the best airlines, fine food preparation and presentation. The aim of the 'micro compact home' and other projects in this group is to bring this concept of high-level products and experiences in a compact environment to earth. The built product is enhanced by the advantages of production in an exceptional family-owned factory in rural Austria. Here the components are fabricated in a clean, sheltered facility with automated quality control that ensures precision in each element. Small-scale foundations and services are prepared on site in parallel with the production process in the factory. When this work is complete it takes just five minutes to install a 'micro compact home'.

SK

SC

SK

micro compact home [m-ch]

Daily life has been transformed by the arrival of technologies such as the internet, flat-screen television, and wireless phones as well as by improvements in domestic appliances like microwave ovens, fridge freezers and LED lights. In addition, building technologies are advancing in the wake of the aerospace, marine and auto industries, enabling new opportunities for living spaces with higher performance and less material. It is now possible to live much better on a much smaller scale. The storage of books was once an essential part of learning or research, and the ownership of objects and rooms to store them an essential expression of wealth. Today we acquire knowledge from the internet and wealth is expressed by a high degree of physical and intellectual mobility. The luxury is in the compact technologies that allow us the greatest freedom of movement. We can now touch and be touched by the world from a tiny space. The 'm-ch' is both luxury and necessity on a small scale, a high-quality home space for short-stay living.

- two compact double beds
- sitting area
- sliding table for work, meetings, dining
- dining space for up to five
- shower
- toilet cubicle
- kitchen area
- fridge and freezer unit
- microwave
- three-bin waste
- double induction hob
- sink and extending tap
- heating
- hot water
- air conditioning
- two flat-screen televisions
- LED lighting
- power sockets
- internet EDV socket
- television aerial socket
- telephone socket
- two mirrors
- shirt cupboard
- storage
- ski store option
- terrace option
- solar cells option

interior

Windows and LED light fittings are positioned to wash work surfaces with light while avoiding the downward glare cast by overhead fixtures. This gives a sense of greater width and overall volume to the spaces. High quality Swiss fittings are used in the kitchen and shower zones with flush units and a minimum of protruding elements to keep the compact space free for movement. The specially selected LED lights cast a warm, natural-like light in the interior avoiding the usual mismatch between daylight and tungsten interior lighting and helping to give a more expansive feeling to the interior by blending with the outdoors.

construction The 'micro compact home' is constructed with a timber frame and panel construction using recyclable and durable flat aluminium cladding. Vacuum insulation is used within the roof composite not only for its thermal efficiency, but to minimize weight. The 'micro compact home' has minimal impact on the environment. Following installation of the support frame onto micro piles the 'm-ch' is crane-installed within five minutes from truck or trailer. Commissioning occurs after connecting the micro compact home to service points. Crane installation allows the 'm-ch' to be positioned with care close to and between trees and within other environmentally sensitive landscapes.

JH

JH

uses

Micro-home villages can be custom-built for sports and leisure while preserving the natural landscape below and around the cubes. They are ideal for skiing or sailing holidays, for yacht clubs needing accommodation for racing crews, for press accommodation at sports and Olympic events, as clusters of mountain huts or for art galleries requiring short-stay space for guest artists, as an urban pied à terre for companies needing visiting staff facilities, for students at universities and boarding schools, for hospital staff or visitors, for trucking companies or airlines needing temporary facilities for returning crews, for short-stay living spaces, for building-site managers and consultants, for teenagers away from home and starter homes for young people who fill their 24-hour day with work and leisure and have minimal domestic requirements. The 'micro compact home' is quality architecture that fulfills a need between permanent and mobile construction, a need between home and hotel, between study and leisure, function and fun.

RH

tree village

Designed primarily for well-landscaped areas for student housing and for business-related pied à terres on tight city sites, the tree village is a vertical arrangement of 'micro compact homes' planned on a minimal 12-m footprint. Its structure is made up of a cluster of structural steel vertical columns or 'reeds' that echo the surrounding natural vertical architecture. This provides an evenly distributed load which reduces the size of foundations and disturbance to tree roots and vegetation. The open central space contains a lift shaft and stairway and supports for 30 micro compact homes. These are serviced with power, water and waste from an internal ring of more vertical 'reeds'. The 'micro compact homes' are arranged around the lift and stair core so as to provide maximum transparency and openness for natural light/views to penetrate the space. A 'micro compact home' can be removed from the tree village by a light crane for maintenance at the production centre without disturbance to the adjacent units.

EO

can touch

O₂

snowboard village

The 'micro compact homes' are raised above the ground providing natural space and airflow between the cube and the ground surface, minimizing foundation disturbance and touching the earth lightly.

The aluminium sub-frames have three legs which are height adjustable to enable the micro homes to be located horizontally on the mountainside. After securing the sub-frame to the slope, the 1.8-tonne micro compact homes are lifted by crane over trees or shrubs. A lighter weight 1.4-tonne unit is available and designed with lifting points for helicopter delivery to remote sites. Space below the 'm-ch' allows the natural landfall and ground surface to be uninterrupted and illuminated at night from the LED light fittings located flush with the underside.

Clean energy for the snowboard village can be provided using solar panels and vertical-axis wind generators. These are mounted on the mast and roof. There is the option of glass-fronted clip-on micro wood-burning stoves that can provide a natural warmth and aroma to enhance the intimate atmosphere inside the home. A storage frame for small logs can be attached to the underside of the cube, as can lockable aluminium containers for skis and snowboards etc., so that nothing clutters the ground and snow surface.

WK

TW

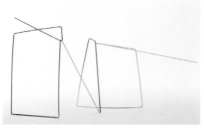

Tango dancers' maquettes by Marijke de Goey

reed huis

The 'reed huis' project is conceived as a small weekend retreat for two, a 'nest in the reeds'. It was developed specifically for the Dutch polder, canal and lakeside landscapes. It was designed in May 2003 by the celebrated Dutch artist Marijke de Goey working with Richard Horden. The tall, reeded sculptures, a development of de Goey's wire maquettes, would be formed with white-painted aluminium tubing and provide a stable three-point support for the 1.8-ton 'micro compact home', creating a 'high-tech nest'. The bent top shape echoes the natural form of windblown reeds. The reeds also provide an identity, like the traditional white bridges or windmills, in the planar Dutch landscape. They function as a support for solar energy panels and wind generator and may be gently illuminated at night with light tubing or up-lights. A second sculptural reed frame provides a light lifting gantry for a small yacht or dinghy, which is pulled clear of the water when not in use.

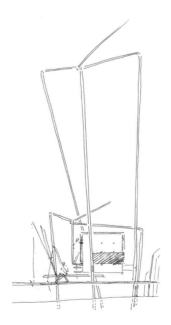

UK 009   In June 2006 the micro compact home
009 was presented for the first time
in Great Britain. Centre of the event
was Berkeley Square in London, only
a stone's throw from the offices of
Horden Cherry Lee. The aim was to
give potential buyers and property de-
velopers the opportunity to experience
'living in the cube' first hand. The same
model has also travelled to Manchester
and to several other countries such as
Austria for the famous downhill skiing
event at Kitzbühel and Switzerland on
special commissions for UBS.

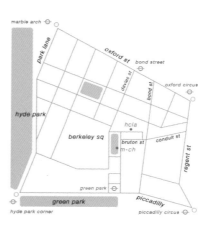

UK 009

The 'micro compact home' is especially designed for 'short-stay smart living'. As a sophisticated, compact accommodation for business or leisure use it is suitable for various locations. Integrated in the smart aluminium cube are sound system, LCD screen, telecommunication and an energy system as well as furniture. The reduced volume of the building creates a fusion with the scale of natural plants and the experience from inside a micro compact home looking out is of a calm compatibility with nature.

Project	Munich, 2005	**Teaching Team**	Prof. Richard Horden
Location	Munich		B. Franke, L. Haack,
Client	Studentenwerk,		H. Müller, A. Vogler,
Students	München e.v.		T. Wessbecher, W. Klasz
	V. Blacker-Sturm, V.	**Architects**	Horden Cherry Lee, London
	Gruber, C. Hainzlmeier,		Haack + Höpfner, Munich
	S. Koch, B. Matern,	**Contractor**	micro compact home
	D. Oswald, M. Penev,		production GmbH
	T. Tuhkanen		

Concept and development: TU Munich, Institute Prof. Richard Horden

European and USA patents: Richard Horden

design team

O₂ village

The first community project of seven micro compact homes was sponsored by O₂ Germany and Siemens for the Studentenwerk, the student housing authority in Munich chaired by Dieter Massberg. The design of the prototype 001 and O₂ village was drawn and supervised by Richard Horden. Architects for the project were Horden Cherry Lee, London, and Haack + Höpfner, Munich. The project was built by the family contractor, Gatterbauer at Uttendorf in Austria. The 'micro compact home' units are arranged along a central walkway raised 50cm above the surrounding lawn and tree landscape. The spaces between the units are the same volume as a single 'micro compact home' and create the feeling of a personal garden outside each unit. The students use these spaces for barbecue parties in summer and for cooking hot chestnuts and *Glühwein* (mulled wine) at Christmas. In winter the snow is illuminated by the time-set lights below the m-ch units.

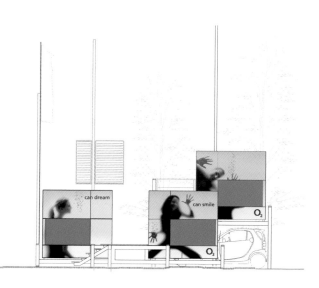

O2

can join

can

ca

can hide

can touch

can laugh

ca

c

SK

design team	**Project**	Munich, 2008
	Location	Central Europe
	Team	Prof. Richard Horden
		Tim Wessbecher

family compact home 01

In 1990 the office in London developed a modular factory-built housing system titled 'skydeck house' with contractors; this was followed in 1999 by the 'city arcade', a project for urban living based on a seven-floor factory-built system with micro habitation units on the roof. The project was designed for the Architecture Foundation Competition 'Living in the City'. At the TU Munich in 2000 a small prefabricated home design was developed by students and known as the 'smart™ home'. There followed a similar project known as the 'starter home' for young families by students. In 2005 we started a collaboration with the TU Delft for an e-ch 'European Concept House', a project still under development by Prof. Mick Eeckhout and Andreas Vogler working in the Netherlands. In 2001 we began the design of 'Tokyo 26'/the 'i-home' later to be called the 'micro compact home'. That unit is now being used as the basis for an exploration of a system for a multi-unit living structure, the family compact home: f-ch.

RH

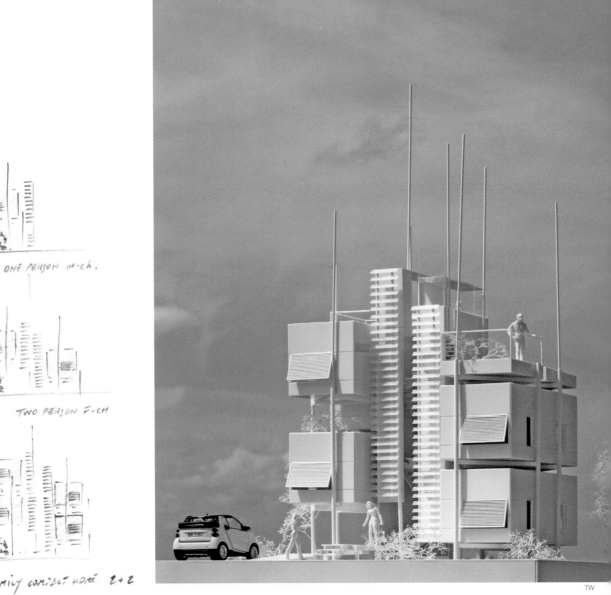

ONE PERSON ra-ch.

TWO PERSON F-CH

FAMILY COMPACT HOME 2+2

TW

Project	Munich, 2008	
	in progress	
Location	Central Europe	
Students	Katharina Kassner	
	Simon Frick	
Teaching Team	Prof. Richard Horden	
	Burkhard Franke	

design team

family compact home 02

The family compact home is based on the 'micro compact home' and explores the potential of organic spaces in a relatively small volume for up to four people. The design strategy of the 'f-ch' is to first imagine the tower as a massive cube and then take organic forms out of it. These negative volumes later become the rooms. The positive that is left over will accommodate circulation spaces. This concept is shown in the first models which were perforated more and more, implying the image of Swiss cheese. Spatially, the project was approached from two sides: on the one hand, organic shapes and rounded edges are applied to create fluent surfaces, referring to car or aircraft interiors which are never sharp-edged but adapted to the contours and movements of the human body. This principle generates the façade. On the other hand, a controlled way of dealing with inexact, organic volumes had to be developed to guarantee a working flow of stairs in the building and a sensible arrangements of rooms.

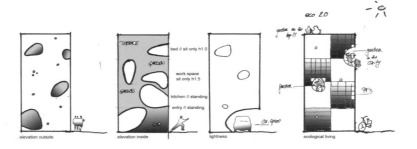

elevation outside | elevation inside | lightness | ecological living

TERRACE
GARDEN
GARDEN

eco 2.0

bed // sit only h1.0

work.space
sit only h1.5

kitchen // standing

entry // standing

garden on the top 2!

garden
in the
cavity

garden

PP's

air.space

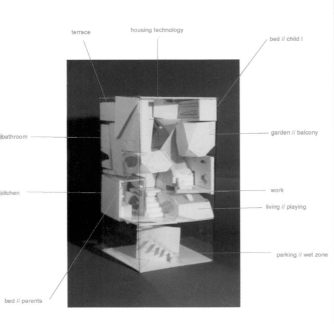

terrace

housing technology

bed // child I

bathroom

garden // balcony

kitchen

work

living // playing

parking // wet zone

bed // parents

design team

Project	Munich, 2008	
	in progress	
Location	Central Europe	
Students	Anna Baumgartner	
	Birgit Neulinger	
Teaching Team	Prof. Richard Horden	
	Walter Klasz	

family compact home 03

The 'wi!-home' is imagined to be the future form of flexible habitation. The 'future family' is changing quickly in constellation and size. Likewise the 'wi!-home' is able to react to any kind of situation and give shelter to patch-work families accommodating senior parents or couples with expanding families.

In our case study we optimized the volume for two adults, two vital seniors and two children. By the concept of piling modules we realized a vertical organization with a small footprint. Spatially the 'wi!-home' is divided into permeable common spaces and closed private capsules. All elements add up to an arrangement of simple compact volumes that can be transported on a truck. The individual module shape is adapted to the spatial needs of the human body to achieve a compact and efficient form. The elevation mimics a folded ribbon and is partly integrated into the common spaces.

wi!-home

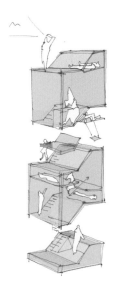

division   common   /   private

Project	Munich, 2008
Location	Solar Decathlon Exhibition, Washington DC
Students	Katharina Kassner
	Simon Frick

Teaching Team	Prof. Richard Horden
	Burkhard Franke

design team

solar pebble

The compact form and the irregular outline of a water-worn pebble provided the idea for this low-energy house project (see also page 198). The absence of any symmetry is one of the key factors for the intriguing shape. A plain surface cut into the curved volume is covered with high performance solar cells. The structure is light, demountable and transportable in six prefabricated modules which fit in a standard ISO container. Since there are no corners, only a single detail is required for the skin. High insulation and low-energy requirements because of the ultra compact use of space also make the building well-suited for use in extreme environments such as very cold or hot regions. A challenging aspect was the design of the organic interior, which is arranged around a central full-height circulation zone, with sitting-only areas at the periphery. The complete project was modelled in 3D and plotted by a rapid prototyping machine.

A 3D plotted physical model and computer renderings were both used to explore the complex 'pebble' shape.

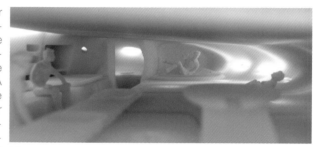

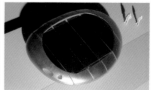

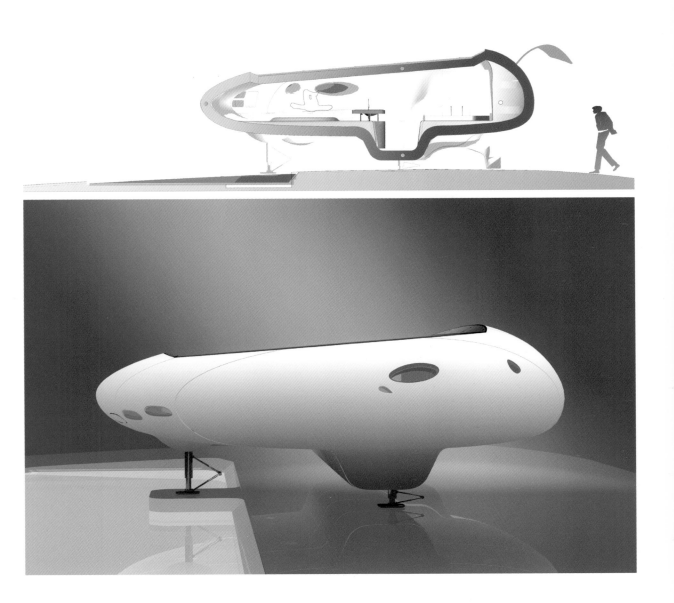

Project	Family compact home, 2007–08	**Teaching Team**	Prof. Richard Horden Walter Klasz
Location	Mobile	**Consultant**	Prof. Gerhard Hausladen Elisabeth Endres
Students	Tjark-Marten Apetz, Philipp Groh		

design team

solar compact home

The Solar Decathlon is a competition in which 20 teams of college and university students compete to design, build, and operate the most attractive, effective, and energy-efficient solar-powered house. The public are also invited to the event to observe the best in solar-powered home design. Today's solar houses are designed to work in connection with nature. They use heat and natural light from the sun, cooling breezes and protective shade. But they improve on this natural advantage by using the newest products and technologies on the market to achieve maximum efficiency. The 'solar compact home' makes use of the solar income with an intelligent shape that follows the path of the sun and maximizes the area of photovoltaic surface directed towards the sun. Furthermore the form optimizes the ratio between volume and surface area.

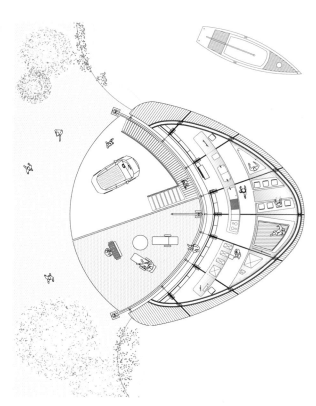

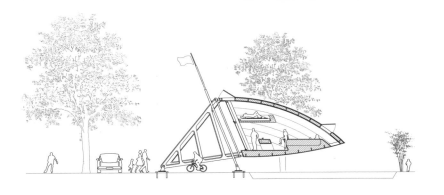

It would be impossible to teach effective design for microgravity without excellent contacts to organizations building and delivering spacecraft. We were fortunate to have guidance from a team of experienced Space designers, engineers and USA and EU astronauts. In 1998 our Institute for Architecture and Product Design teamed with the Faculty for Aerospace led by Prof. Eduard Igenbergs, who had developed and launched a satellite programme for deep space research, and Hans Huber, designer of the Munich Space Chair [MSC] which had been tested on the MIR Space Station in 1995 and later launched to the International Space Station [ISS] in August 2007, where it is now in constant use. Later we teamed with Constance Adams from Lockheed Martin, Houston, and NASA's team from Building Nine (the ISS and Space Shuttle Training Building) at the Johnson Space Center in Houston who allowed our students and team to use the Electronic classroom there for design development and presentations. Our four student groups were privileged to have one week of microgravity test flights from NASA's Ellington Field near Houston and interaction on their designs with NASA engineers and astronauts.

aerospace

microgravity projects

International Space Station ISS, seen from Space Shuttle Endeavour, on 24 March 2008

NASA

design team

Project	Munich, 1998–2004	**Engineers**	Prof. E. Igenbergs, Dept. for Astronautics,
Location	NASA		TU-München, Hans Huber
Students	B. Artopé, Björn		Ernst K. Pfeiffer, Keyser-Threde
	Betheau, B. Borst	**Consultants**	Prof. H. Baier, TU-Munich
	Th. Dirlich, J. Habel,		Prof. H. Bubb, TU-Munich
	C. Hertrich, A. Hof-	**Sponsors**	Alu–Meier, Munich
	mann, S. Hoffmann,		Brück Leichtbautechnik
	Ch. Hooff, A. Laub,		Hans Grohe, Schiltach
	C. Pöppel		Horbach Werbetechnik, Munich
Teaching Team	Prof. Richard Horden		Käthe Kruse, Donauwörth
	Lydia Haack		Rosner Lacke, Munich
	Andreas Vogler		Schreinerei Gleissner & Stevens, Munich
NASA Team	Constance Adams		Specken Drumag, Bad Säckingen
	David Fitts		Vontana Wasserbetten, Oererckenschwig
	Nathan Moore	**Funding**	Bayern Innovativ
	David Ray		Bund Der Freunde Der TU Munich

microgravity projects

In collaboration with the department for astronautics at the university of technology in Munich (TU Munich) and NASA's Johnson Space Center in Houston, our department has been conducting a number of microgravity projects since the autumn of 1998.

With the erection of the International Space Station, long-term stays in space will become a routine event. This poses the question of the habitable quality of a space station. The extreme demands made of astronauts require an ideal environment for work and relaxation. The main emphasis of the microgravity projects lies in the formulation of design criteria for the functional organization of workplaces and leisure areas in the International Space Station.

Individual groups are drawing up proposals for standardized sanitary, sleeping and living racks within the habitation module. These proposals are being tested by means of full-size mock-ups. A presentation to NASA was so successful that they offered to

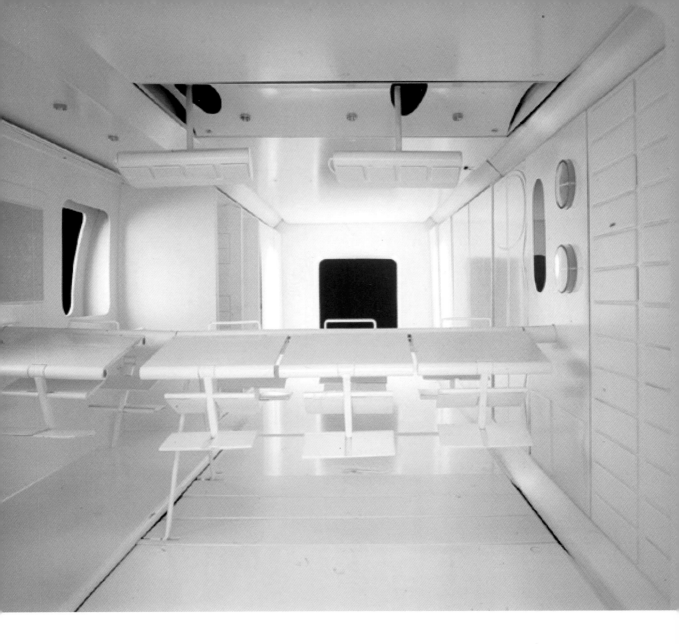

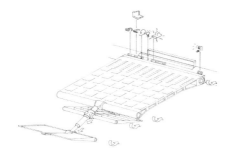

organize a series of kc135 parabolic flights to test the designs under conditions of microgravity.

The microgravity projects offer a splendid opportunity for a transdisciplinary collaboration between a wide range of experts as well as a cooperation with the space industry. Exchanges between our designers and NASA are taking place via the internet and video conferences. They provide an opportunity to plan in accordance with real needs and technologies. Regular discussions with the German astronaut Reinhold Ewald reveal the user's point of view.

The synergetic potential of space architecture lies in a fundamental rethinking of the processes of planning and design under conditions of microgravity, and in becoming conversant with complex links between systems. The outcome is an enormous potential for new ideas and spin-off developments, which may also find an application in terrestrial architecture.

Space shower: combining water pressure with suction permits the controlled use of fresh water in a space craft.

Our tall building strategy is to examine the unique qualities of super-high buildings above 500m. We have developed areas of special innovation at our Institute and in the teaching at the ETH Zurich that have to do with wind and solar energy and cool-air collection. We are especially interested in the possibilities of cable-car access to super-high buildings, a solution that offers the advantages of increased safety in escape and of distributing access for people and goods over a wider footprint. This reduces the wasted plan area taken up by the many elevators, a factor which also causes extreme congestion at the base of high buildings.

tall buildings

eurotower | european expo tower

Sky over *Dreiländereck*, Germany, France, Switzerland

AvP

design team

Project	Munich, 2003	Teaching Team	Prof. Richard Horden
Location	Dreiländereck, Basel		Burkhard Franke
Students	Georg Glas	Consultant	A. Pernpeintner, TUM
	Ulrich Egger		Prof. R. Barthel, TUM
	Julian Hildebrand		
	Fabian Matthes		
	Georg Rötzel		
	Minh N. Thai		
	Stefan Winter		

eurotower

These two high-rise towers have been designed for the *Dreiländereck* near Basel, where Germany, France and Switzerland meet. Measuring 650m and 1,000m in height, both projects examine the impact of extremely high structures on the European city. Both projects are partly accessed by cable cars. This 'servicing through air' avoids the usual spatial and static problems at the tower's foot point which can be held free and open. Both towers only slightly touch the earth. On the other hand the cable-car stations can become the centres of activity, at the mid points of the towers. This way the towers become a connecting element over the borders of three countries, a hub, where people from different nations work, live and exchange information. This function as an 'information filter' best expresses the character of such a significant building at the beginning of a new millennium.

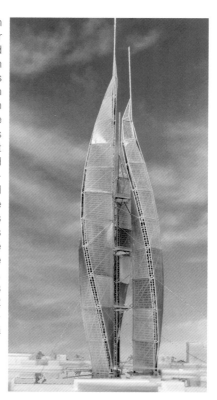

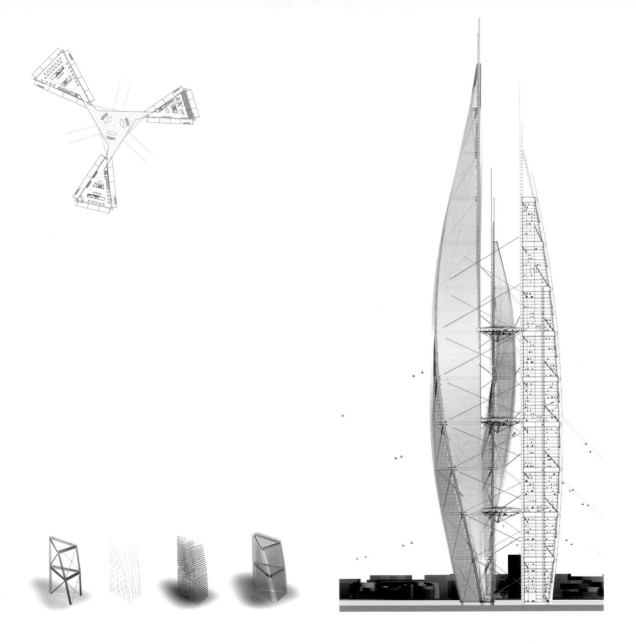

Project	Munich, 2003	**Teaching Team**	Prof. Richard Horden
Location	Dreiländereck, Basel		Burkhard Franke
Students	Fabian Gärtner	**Consultant**	A. Pernpeintner, TUM
	Christian von Sieg		Prof. R. Barthel, TUM
	Vitus Straehuber		
	Rodrigo Uzquiano		
	Andreas Walther		
	Arndt Weiss		
	Stefan Winter		

design team

european expo tower

The former container harbour of Basel is separated from the Rhine by an artificial island, which is pointing towards the *Dreiländereck* or 'three corners'. Three directions, heading from the *Dreiländereck* to each country, form a triangular grid, which defines the urban structure on the island and in the harbour. The 'european expo tower' grows at the top of the former island out of the grid. With an overall height of 1,120 metres and a highest accessible floor at 1,000 metres, it offers three cable-car stations which are arranged around the tower, each in one country. They connect to the Basel-Mulhouse Airport, the city centre of Basel and the German–Swiss border. The tower has two main stations where the cable cars arrive and depart. The platforms above the stations are continuous areas and are arranged at a height of 335m and 495m. The vertical city of the 'european expo tower' offers a huge variety of functions to facilitate and enhance working and living.

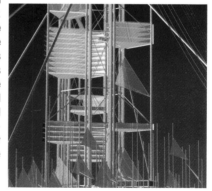

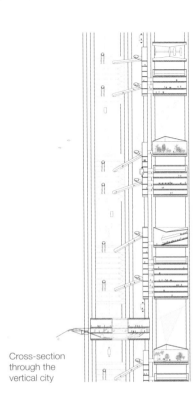

Cross-section
through the
vertical city

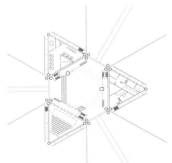

Floorplan of the mixed-
use neighbourhood

Bridges were once the domain of engineers, but architects have become more involved in bridge design in recent years. Like tall buildings they are largely surrounded by free space, a condition that offers special aesthetic and technical opportunities which architects love to explore. Today bridge buildings or 'living bridges' present opportunities for natural cooling and reduced energy consumption in the habitable structures attached to them by taking advantage of the cooling effects from the river or ground water below, or from the lower surrounding air temperature. These make them especially attractive as highly visible models for new low-carbon-emission design. Living bridges can be constructed using very efficient, large-scale prefabrication due to the fact that delivery can often be made from the river, so that construction can be completed with minimum disruption to congested city streets. In 2004 Horden Cherry Lee Architects made a proposal to the mayor of London for a monorail that would travel along the River Thames. The project would be a highly visible modern addition to the city and would provide service to and from London's key landmarks and the 2012 Olympic site. For this large project too, delivery and construction could be made very efficient by using the river to transport large prefabricated sections.

bridges

Dubai souq bridge | seagull bridge | auberge du vedon | tensegrity bridge

Blue Lake Caumasee, Flims, Switzerland   RH

design team

Project	Munich, 2002	**Teaching Team**	Prof. Richard Horden
Location	Dubai Creek		Andreas Vogler
Students	Sabine Kunzfeld		
	Jacob Plötz		

Dubai souq bridge

This award-winning S-shaped design for a pedestrian bridge spans Dubai Creek connecting two old parts of town. The 'graining' (small units) of the adjacent souk markets is reflected in the small connective shop units on the bridge. Adjustable 'wind scoops' mounted alongside the bridge serve as sunshades and direct cool winds from the water surface on to the bridge. Like white sails they enliven and lighten the appearance and give the impression of a passing regatta.

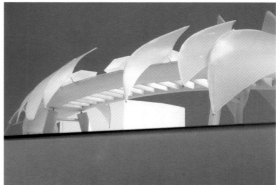

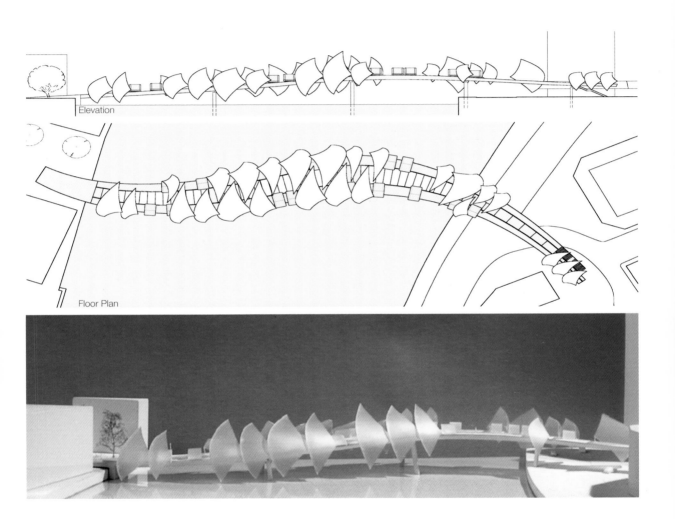

Elevation

Floor Plan

Project	Munich, 2002	**Teaching Team**	Prof. Richard Horden
Location	Barcelona		Burkhard Franke
Students	Georg Glas,		
	Julian Hildebrand		

design team

seagull bridge

Bridges and towers are architecture in free space and it is not only the structural elegance but the point of contact with the earth that is the critical, technical and visual *Schwerpunkt* which means literally 'heavy point' or key issue.

The 'seagull bridge', a pedestrian-only bridge, solves the problem by having one point of rotation in the centre of the waterway for shipping within Barcelona harbour. Inspired by the way the wing tip of a seabird seems to caress the water as it makes a turn, the free ends of the bridge take on a wing-like form. The lower wing tip becomes the point of contact, floating just over the land with a step-up access point for travellers and visitors. The high point is the counterbalance. The central support is also useful as a separation and channel marker for shipping travelling in opposite directions, and the raised counterweight side with its visitor centre allows smaller boats to pass below it uninterrupted at any time.

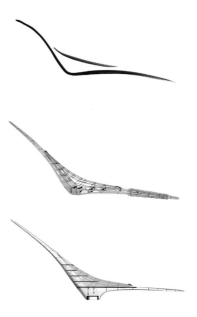

design team

Project   Munich, 2002
Location   Verdon
Students   Frieder Lohmann
            Tobias Mattes

Teaching Team   Prof. Richard Horden
                   Birgitta Kunsch

auberge du verdon

A shaped tube can make an excellent bridge form. This design creates a bridge and visitor centre within a polished aluminium-clad steel frame tube. Two points of contact on either side of the gorge provide the lateral stability and the third point takes the majority of the weight on to a rock ledge below and close to the river. The silver-polished aluminium and glass finish also reflects the surrounding rock formations.

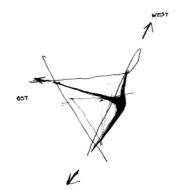

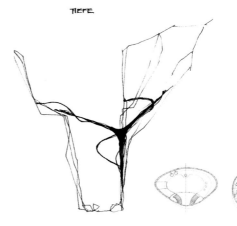

design team

Project	Copenhagen, 1998	**Teaching Team**	Prof. Richard Horden
Location	River Thames, London		Karin Skousbøll
Students	Søren Aagaard		Andreas Vogler
	Susy Carolin Baasel	**Materials**	Aluminium
	Gudrun Holzer		
	Ng Gin Ling		
	Michael Woodford		

tensegrity bridge

The brilliant work of American sculptor Kenneth Snelson inspired a study into the construction of a tensegrity 'sport bridge' across the canals of Copenhagen. We had worked with Kenneth Snelson – a student of Buckminster Fuller and originator of the tensegrity principle of 'floating compression' – on a design for a tensegrity bridge across the Thames. This work has been an inspiration for our projects since my first visit to one of his exhibitions in Bryant Park, New York, in 1968. The students worked intensely under the guidance of Karin Skousbøll and achieved a polished 1/20 scale model of the bridge. The final design would weigh approximately 1 ton.

In 1996 RHA proposed a design together with Kenneth Snelson for a floating compression pedestrian bridge linking St. Paul's with the new Tate Gallery in London.

Being a yachtsman, I have always found polished aluminium a pleasure to touch; it is warmer
than steel or stainless steel and its lightness and
relative softness are perceptable through the fin-
gers. This is largely why we have developed all of
our fittings for interior use in aluminium. The first
'aerospace' tables were designed in aluminium
and acrylic for my own home. I wanted my
family to enjoy lightness and transparency but
without the hazard of sharp heavy glass edges
which would be a great risk to children. The
acrylic tops are warm to the touch, so drawing
on that surface is much more sensual than on
glass. Aluminium and acrylic also complement
one another in weight and softness, and both
scratch a little with age, which I feel adds to the
character of the materials. I designed the door
handle 'aeros', which we used in the Queen's
Stand and recently in the home 'South Deep' on
Poole Harbour, with Sarah Waller from our office.
The design was influenced by a handle created
by Oliver Hill at 'Landfall', which is a stones
throw from 'South Deep'. The basic square
aluminium office table system which I designed
in 1985 is now used in our London office and at
the TU Munich where I was also asked to design
a display system for the University. The result
was 'system 26', which is framed in aluminium
tubing. The system is still evolving into a wide-
ranging furniture system based on a simple joint
that has a close relationship to the Fritz Haller
stainless-steel USM system, and has also inspired development work at Foster and Partners.

interiors

aerospace table | graphite chair | twisty table | system 26 | modular display system | aeros door handle

'twisty table', aluminium and acrylic

EO

aerospace table

The idea for the aluminium and carbon extrusions used for the frame and legs of the aerospace tables came from the yacht industry. The large conference table is 3 x 1 x 0.65m high and makes use of the mechanism of spreaders (the horizontal oval tubes that keep the rigging cables spread away from the mast) from an Americas' Cup yacht mast. The table is relatively light, thanks to the acrylic used for the table tops, which maintains transparency but is also warmer to the touch than glass. The X shape of the support frame was informed by the axle of a sports car and creates a narrow waist and focal point at the centre that also recalls the female form. The table has been produced in smaller dining tables and as low tables (0.45m high). The small tables are built from the aluminium and carbon spreader sections from a 505 Olympic-class dinghy. The tables were built at Sparcraft in Lymington, on the south coast of England, who were also the contractors for the 'ski haus' and 'point lookout'.

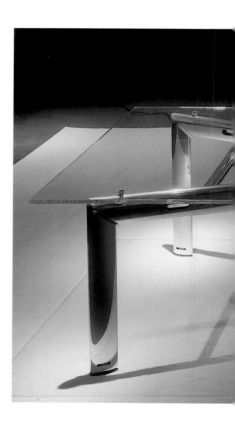

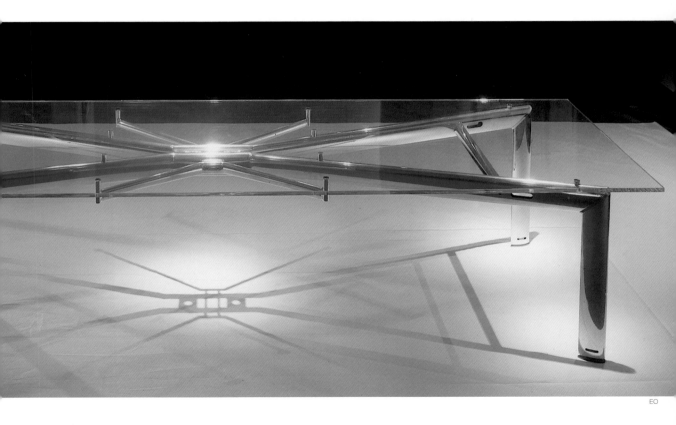

EO

aerospace table | 289

Project	London, 1989
Location	mobile object
Team	Richard Horden Associates

EO

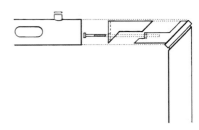

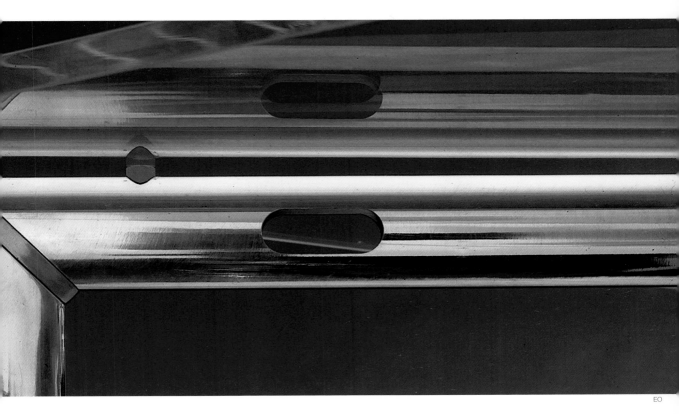

aerospace table | 291

Project	London, 1989
Location	mobile object
Team	Richard Horden Associates

design team

graphite chair

The 'graphite chair' is inspired by the lightweight quality of the modern carbon tennis racket. Our design objective was to achieve a high-design folding chair for use in home, office, café or sporting events; something light, compact and 'baggable' like the tennis racket. The furniture series for this product is titled 'aerospace group' because the early prototypes were developed with engineers from Britain's Concorde and Rolls Royce aerospace factories. The assembly was done by Amalgam model-makers, and by builders of satellite mock-ups for the British aerospace industry. The tables of the 'aerospace' series form a range from small (1-metre) square or round to larger study, dining and conference sizes. They are detailed to be flat-packed and the light weight makes them suitable for bulk air-freighting. The aluminium or carbon-fibre construction makes them durable for outside use. The furniture series is a further step towards 'lightening' our environment.

1/4 scale model of the 'graphite chair'. The office variant comes with silver frame and light grey vinyl fabric; the café, 'yacht' and tennis chairs with acrylic canvas

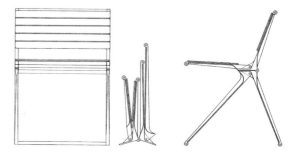

graphite chair | 293

design team

Project   Munich, 2004   **Consultants**   Tim Wessbecher
Location   mobile object   Werner Olschok
                                                                Alu Meier

Team   Prof. Richard Horden

twisty table

These are a development of the basic shape of the aerospace tables. Two advantages accrue by twisting the aluminium bar that forms the support frame and legs: firstly the twist in the horizontal plane makes the central support part deeper and therefore stronger, secondly the twist means that the legs of the table are stiffer in the transverse direction. Both the 'twisty tables' and the 'aerospace tables' require light cross bracing in some form to the ends of the tables to prevent rocking due to the lightness and relative softness of aluminium. A third product of the twist is the sparkle and reflections that shine from the highly polished curved surface of the aluminium. This surface will last a very long time if the tables are used internally or in dry, low-salt climates.

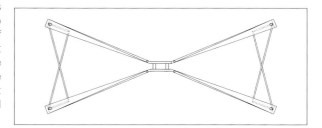

RH

twisty table | 295

The aluminium frame embraces the
'Alusuisse' panels, no fixings required.
The compact corner knuckle gives 'design
freedom' to add lights, shelves and storage
units. The objective: simplicity in assembly.

system 26

I had designed a very light aluminium table for our office in London and brought the same product to the University when I began teaching in 1996. Our Institute was invited by the TU Munich to design an exhibition system for the University for diploma presentations as well for conferences and displays. I had been a great supporter and specifier of the Swiss USM storage system designed by Fritz Haller in the 1960s, which is made in stainless steel, and specified its use in a number of architectural projects that I worked on. This opportunity provided me with a chance to find a lighter and more easily assembled system both for the University and for the office in London.

'System 26' uses a 26-mm diameter aluminium tube and corner connectors to make freestanding display panels and a variety of tables, as well as an easy to use stackable storage system, lights, chairs and other accessories. In 1985 I had been working with Jan Kaplicky for Norman Foster on a storage system to complement his suc-cessful 'Nomos' glass tables. A design later emerged and I wrote to Norman Foster suggesting I pick up the design and continue it for the University.

'System 26' is the result of that design process, and we are now expanding it for use in our new office in Berkeley Square, London.

Project	Munich, 1996	**Consultants**	Tim Wessbecher
Location	mobile objects		Werner Olschok
			Alu Meier
Team	Prof. Richard Horden		

design team

'System 26';
LED light fixed to the
system connections

TW

EO

system 26 | 299

Project	Munich, 1997–98	**Consultants**	Bartenbach Lichtlabor Gmbh
Location	TU Munich	**Sponsors**	Alu-Meier, Munich
Students	Michaela Hoppe		
	Christopher von		
	der Howen		
	Eva Neumeyer		
Teaching Team	Prof. Richard Horden		
	Andreas Vogler		
	Lydia Haack		

design team

modular display system

The development of a display system, together with the redesign of the entrance hall, a CAD (Computer Aided Design) pool and exhibition space, is one of a series of projects undertaken by the department to improve the appearance of the TU Munich. In addition to the need to meet functional requirements and to guarantee stability and reliability, the furniture system was to reflect the precision and aesthetics of modern engineering sciences. The design is based on a framework of anodized aluminium tubes, jointed with double-wedge connectors, and used in conjunction with aluminium composite panels. The furniture can be quickly assembled or dismantled by hand with a few basic tools, and can be stored in a space-saving form. The series comprises all units required for use in a modern university.

The 'Alusuisse' alucore panels are held in place by the aluminium tubes

Detail foot

RH

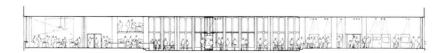

prototypes of
exhibition panels

RH

design team

Project England, 1992
Location Queen's Stand,
Epsom, England
RHA Office, London
House, Hampstead,
London
House on Evening Hill,
Poole
Design Team Prof. Richard Horden
Sarah Kirby
Billie Lee

RH

aeros door handle

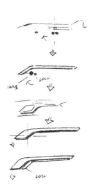

A simple flat lengthened aluminium profile was used for the Queen's Stand door handle, in order to achieve a design compatible with the flat profiles of the stairways and balcony viewing rails.

The door handle was designed for use in the 'Queen's Stand' (see page 22) and is also informed by the elegant, splayed forms of yachts, helicopters and the Concorde. With Sarah Waller from our office I designed the 'aeros door handle' which we used in the Queen's Stand and recently in the home 'South Deep' on Poole Harbour. It was influenced by the design of a handle by Oliver Hill at 'Landfall', (see photo above), close to 'South Deep'. The handle can be operated from either side because the lever tilts beyond the rocker point (see sketches to the side). The handle provides an 'active' position for the thumb as well as the palm, which is unusual in lever-handle design. The 'aeros' is the first of a series of aluminium and stainless-steel products, produced and distributed by Elementer Industrial Design Ltd., England.

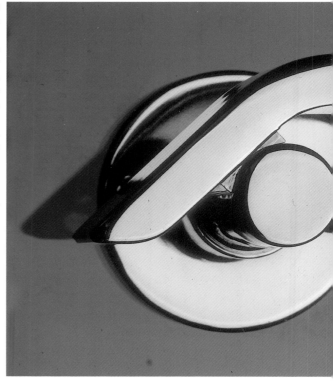

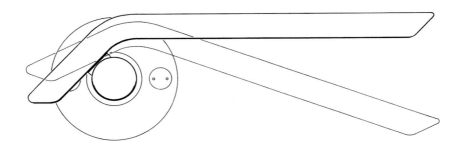

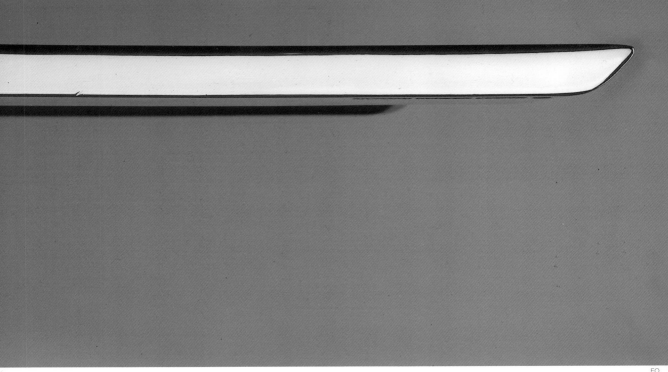

EO

aeros door handle | 303

micro architecture | appendix

selected projects
by richard horden

Richard Horden studied at the Architectural Association from 1964 to 1969. He worked for Spence & Webster Architects and Foster Associates (1975–85), before starting his own practice, Richard Horden Associates, in 1985. He began teaching micro architecture at the TU Munich in 1996. His current London office, Horden Cherry Lee, was opened in 1999 with Stephen Cherry and Billie Lee.

Many of the young people who have studied at our Institute at the Technical University in Munich come to work at our London practice and for Foster and Partners, where the ethos of openness and transparency is the primary aim for the clients' projects and for the architectural composition. The philosophy of lightness, transparency and 'touching the earth lightly' is reinterpreted in our larger urban designs and in the smaller scale private domestic buildings in England. Some of the concepts and micro architecture projects developed at the TU Munich are a direct influence on some of our larger scale designs. For example, the micro compact home/reed huis project helped inform the 45-floor Park Place office building which expresses the original natural reeded landscape of the river banks at the Docklands on the Thames.

We strive for both visual and physical lightness, studying the effect of light on form, the aesthetics of light and colour and lightness in relation to energy and the environment to generate an architecture that is both calm and uplifting for society and the environment.

A first student project at the AA in 1964.
Today we build these 2.6cm 'nano' cubes as gifts for the students who live in the micro compact homes in the O_2 Village.

Courtyard House
1974, Poole
Richard Horden

Yacht House
1983, New Forest
Richard Horden, Peter Horden

Parliamentary Building
1972, Westminster, London
Winning design for an International Competition, Spence & Webster Architects
Richard Horden, Jan Kaplicky, Hugh Morgan, Robin Spence, Robin Webster

Stansted Airport
Stansted
work for Norman Foster

Sainsbury Centre for the Visual Arts
1978, Norwich
work for Norman Foster

Ski Haus
1991
Ken Boyd, Richard Horden, Sarah Kirby, Brian Kelly

East Circular Quai
1992, Competition, Sydney
Sarah Forbes Waller, Richard Horden, Russell Jones, Sarah Kirby, Susan Mclean, Brian McClymont

Glass Cubes
1992, Project, London
Alan Grant, Richard
Horden, Sarah Kirby,
Michael Wigginton

Swiss-Air Tower
1993, Project
Sarah Forbes Waller,
Richard Horden, Sarah
Kirby, Sarah North

Point Lookout
1993, Australia
Sarah Forbes Waller,
Russell Jones, Richard
Horden, Sarah Kirby

Queen's Stand
1993, Epsom Downs, Surrey
C. Cheney, S. Forbes Waller, A. Grant,
R. Horden, C. Hislop, Th. Höger, R. Jones,
S. Kirby, S. Krüger, B. Lee, E. Martin,
B.Mcclymont, S. McClean, D. Reid, M. Sedel-
mayer, O. Stirling, J. Wilson, M. Wigginton

Folding Canopies
1994, London
Mira Esposito, Sarah
Forbes Waller, Richard
Horden, Brian Kelly,
Billie Lee, Sarah North

St. Marks Hospital
1995, London
Sarah Forbes Waller,
Kathy Horden, Richard
Horden, Sarah Kirby,
Billie Lee, Sarah North

The Study Gallery
1997, Poole
Mira Esposito, Richard
Horden, Ben Knight,
Billie Lee, Tom Roberts,
Jeremy Main, Raj
Suresh Narputharaj

Marine Tower
1997, Project, Poole
Richard Horden,
Billie Lee

Wing Tower
2001, Realisation
Glasgow
Peter Heppel, Richard
Horden, Billie Lee

House on Poole Harbour
2002
Mira Esposito, Richard
Horden, Billie Lee, Peter
Ludwig, Sarah Kirby

Ercol Furniture Factory
2002
Stephen Blowers, Stephen Cherry, David
Franklin, Pascal Gysi, Rainer Hofmann, Richard
Horden, Billie Lee, Peter Ludwig, Kwamina
Monney, Manon Stockhammer

Finsbury Square
Royal Bank of Scotland
2004
Richard Horden, Billie
Lee, Stephen Cherry,
David Franklin, Manon
Stockhammer, Matthew
Williams, Claudia
Hertrich, Tina Reschke

London Office
2004
Stephen Cherry, Richard Horden, Billie Lee

Micro Compact Home [0$_2$ village]
2005, Munich,
with Haack + Höpfner Architekten, Munich
V. Blacker-Sturm, B. Franke, V. Gruber, L. Haack,
C. Hainzlmeier, R. Horden, W. Klasz, S. Koch,
B. Matern, H. Müller, D. Oswald, M. Penev,
W. Seidler, T. Tuhkanen, A. Vogler, T. Wessbecher

Tulip Tower, Amsterdam
2006
Design Study for KPN
The Netherlands
Marijke de Goey
Richard Horden AGS/
Scwencke Rosbach
Tim Wessbecher

10 Chiswell Street
Offices for Fairplay Est.
2007
Richard Horden, Billie
Lee, Stephen Cherry,
David Franklin, Tina
Reschke, Matthew
Williams

Poole Waterfront
Museum
2007
Ulrike Fuchs, Richard
Horden, Tina Resche,
Billie Lee

30 Crown Place
London
City Offices Real Estate
2008
Richard Horden,
Stephen Cherry, Manon
Stockhammer,
Matthew Williams,
Karoline Lochbrunner,
Hanna Nasfeter, Ulrike
Fuchs, Con Karlos,
Georg Rötzel

Chelsea Barracks
2007, London
Richard Horden,
Stephen Cherry, Ulrike
Fuchs, Katherine
Goddard

NZ Solar Bridge
2008
Auckland Harbour
Competition
Ulrike Fuchs, Marijke de
Goey, Richard Horden,
Tim Wessbecher,
Josef Musil

Park Place
Docklands, London
2008
Richard Horden,
Stephen Cherry, Billie
Lee, David Franklin,
Ulrike Fuchs, Yosuke
Komiyama, Richard
Evans, Chrystal Lau,
Katharina Fleck

Riverside Apartments on the Embankment
2008, London
Richard Horden, Stephen Cherry, Tina
Reschke, David Franklin, Ulrike Fuchs, Simona
Rossi, Sherman Tang, Sebastian Uhl, Henry Rist,
Fabio Wendnagel

House in Cornwall
2008
Richard Horden, Billie
Lee, Yuki Namba,
Sebastian Uhl

appendix

exhibition at MoMA

The micro compact home was included in a major architectural exhibition at The Museum of Modern Art, in New York, July–October, 2008.

'Home Delivery: Fabricating the Modern Dwelling' offers the most thorough examination of the historical and contemporary significance of factory-produced architecture to date. With increasing concern about such issues as sustainability and the swelling global population, prefabrication has taken centre stage as a prime solution to a host of pressing needs. The viability of prefabricated structures has long served as a central precept in modern architecture, and it continues to spur imaginative design and the development of innovative manufacturing processes. The exhibition features five full-scale contemporary prefabricated houses, to be constructed in the outdoor space to the west of the main museum building, continuing MoMA's rich history of presenting full-scale architectural projects.

The Museum of Modern Art [MoMA], designed by Yoshio Taniguchi. Entrance at 53rd Street.

MoMA

The following blogs were posted on the MoMA website in anticipation of the Home Delivery exhibition.

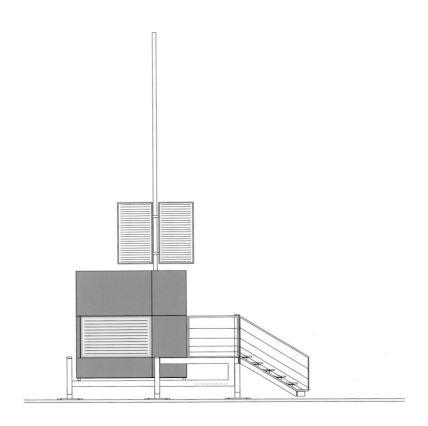

MICRO COMPACT HOME: FROM AVIATION TO ARCHITECTURE
by Richard Horden

blog nr. 1

With hindsight, it is clearer now more than ever that the origin of the micro compact home is from my own peculiar observations of aviation. In fact, since our delightful flights in the Jet Ranger 'Whisky Mike' with Norman Foster in the 1980s, and flights in the Aerospatiale Lama helicopter with Swiss alpine pilots (who have delivered our 'Ski Haus' project to the high mountains since the early 1990s), I realize that most of our projects have indeed been informed by the many links between aviation and architecture.

Aviation is inbuilt with a need for precision. This precision is not only to do with the essential technical aspects, but is carried through the industry to influence everything from airline graphic design, crew presentation, cutlery design, communication, airport design and, in the best airlines, elegant new ideas in food preparation and presentation. We can learn from techniques in minimizing waste in material, food consumption and fuel. I was interested to see a recent brochure from Lufthansa and Swissair, carefully outlining that aviation uses only 1.6 per cent of our total world carbon emissions [source: World Resources Institute], and the industry will no doubt be fast to shift to zero fossil fuels.

Today I am fortunate to experience regular weekly drives in Swissair Smart cars and flights with the highest quality airlines, such as Swissair and Lufthansa, over the Alps between Zurich and Munich. These experiences have engendered a strong appreciation and inspiration for the delight of design quality that accompanies the best aviation experiences – fine graphics, such as those by Tyler Bruleé, and the combination of great products and digital presentation that fit perfectly with the taut and elegant design of the Zurich and Munich airports. Herr Sander-Carqueville, the director of the pure white Munich Airport (voted best airport in Europe for the past three years), explained his philosophy to me as 'seamless travel'. Quality design and architecture is always underpinned by care and precision in thinking and realization.

Precision is at the heart of the design of the micro compact home – in human scale and product design, in colour, LED lighting, minimal energy use, and detailing, and in precisely zoning the four principal human functions: sleep, hygiene, food preparation and work. We sometimes call it an instrument for living, like a Swiss watch – compact function and beauty are integral to the product.

appendix

'Ski Haus', a first micro-architecture project. Helicopter delivery of a 'Ski Haus' to the Swiss-Italian ridge at 3,980m, near Zermatt, 2005.

RH

The Aerospatiale Lama helicopter returns to Zermatt after delivering the 'Ski Haus'

RH

... Friday, 04 April 2008

THE QUEEN'S STAND AND THE MICRO COMPACT HOME
by Richard Horden

blog nr. 2

In 1991, the team at my office in London had been involved in the design of some large buildings in England, in particular the Queen's Stand at Epsom Racecourse. The project had to be built to a very tight programme and could not interrupt any of the horse-racing events, in particular the Derby on the first Saturday in June, one, if not *the* most important event in the international season. The existing building had to be demolished and the new one built for 5,000 champagne-sipping racegoers.

The pressure to deliver the project efficiently was even more than usual as Queen Elizabeth and members of the Royal Family attend every year. The Queen has her own suite of rooms and balcony on the building. One of the most essential ways to achieve a fast build is to construct components off-site and reduce the problems on site to a simple assembly process, as much as possible. This meant that all balconies, cladding, and roof elements needed to be prefabricated. I was fascinated by the petite scale of the oldest structure on the course, the Prince's Stand, which was located just to the west of the site for the new building. The relatively small scale of the balcony and roof on this charming building had, I felt, a perfect scale that should be echoed in the new building.

We presented the design drawings, models, and mock-ups to Sir Evelyn de Rothschild and the Queen in the Picture Gallery at Buckingham Palace with a strong instruction to proceed. The experience of reducing the building elements to a minimum proved very effective and the project was completed on time for Derby Day 1993 ... and for a very happy client!

As a designer, I enjoyed the regular factory visits to check the balcony detailing, quality, and progress and it seemed to me a delightful way to build. In my mind, micro architecture was born then, and not only as an effective and fast building method but as a teaching tool to help young architectural students to design and manage their own projects. Later the press and television interview point on the Queen's Stand was to directly influence 'Point Lookout' in Australia, garden canopies for Buckingham Palace, and other viewpoint projects by Richard Horden Associates and those at my Institute at the TU Munich, begun in 1996, which we now refer to as 'micro architecture'. Ten years later the micro compact home is, for me, a direct descendent of the Queen's Stand, but this time complete building delivery is in five minutes!

DG

HCLA

RH

TUM

JH

MICRO ARCHITECTURE: LESS MATERIAL, MORE NATURE
by Richard Horden

blog nr. 3

My first opportunity to teach 'micro architecture' came when Peter McCleary called from the Graduate School of Architecture at the University of Pennsylvania in 1990. The invitation was to make a guest teaching programme over two terms.

I had established a small office in central London with a good foundation of work, so the possibility of taking time out to teach for a series of short visits to Philadelphia was appealing. We had won several major international competitions since the Parliamentary Building win in 1974 and I had spent spent ten hard-working and highly informative years at Foster Associates before starting the office.

There was a real desire to develop some experimental ideas, essentially to find a way to bring intense office practice directly to students, as, for example, Craig Ellwood had worked and built with students from UCLA and The Art Centre College on the Bridge House, among other projects. The task was to compact modern architectural theory, practice, and building into a two-semester programme; this could only be done with small-scale projects, a kind of 'architecture simulator'. Flying in on the approach to JFK and Philadelphia in the cockpit of a 747 with friend, Captain Mauleverer, I was inspired by the landscape of forests and rivers, inlets and islands. So the first project we set was for a compact rugged retreat that could be installed by truck or a light helicopter.

The task in 'micro architecture' teaching is to engage with the students to achieve 'less material and more nature'. Students had to select their own sites, in this case on Wissahickon Creek on the outer west side of Philadelphia, and then develop a project that optimized their chosen landscape and natural light. After the first-term presentations, Peter McCleary acquired funds for the material and construction of prototypes, and students teamed up to build and install a selected shortlist of designs on the sites.

One of these was a light fishing platform which could be lifted into place in varying locations. This gave the graduate students a full, if high-speed, experience and insight into the process of design, construction, and installation, as well as in handling the production problems of a full-scale, proof-of-concept prototype. This prepared them for what was to follow ... the 'Ski Haus'.

Two graduate students, Ken Boyd and Brian Kelly, came to our office in London. They worked intensively for three months and designed and supervised the construction of the 'Ski Haus' while working in the yacht factory at Sparcraft in Lymington in the New Forest close to Poole. The students had then experienced the full design process from sketches to factory construction and delivery to Switzerland. The 'Ski Haus' project, completed in 1991, was closely followed by 'Point Lookout' in Australia for students in Adelaide in 1992 and the canopies for Buckingham Palace in 1994.

Today the same principles underlie our teaching programme at the TU Munich, although technology has moved on and with it demands for reduced energy and CO_2 emissions, as well as material reduction. The inspiration has also evolved from the hang glider to the i-phone, laptop, and now the emerging lightweight compact space travel which Burt Rutan has developed in the Rutan VariEze and the Virgin Galactic Space Shuttle.

RH

RH

RH

... Friday, 18 April 2008

THE JOURNEY TO MoMA
by Richard Horden

blog nr. 4

The 'Home Delivery' exhibition at MoMA in July 2008 will be the first appearance of the micro compact home in the USA. It is built in Austria at a family-run factory outside the small village of Uttendorf, roughly 30 miles north of Salzburg.

As I write this, the m-ch is being assembled and prepared for the 4,000-mile journey by directors of micro compact home production Ltd, Nicole and Rupert Gatterbauer, and their team. They are used to travelling with the m-ch and to providing the care required to protect the high-quality insulating glass windows, precision fit-out, and aluminium supporting frame. A 104.3-inch (265-cm) cube, the home is entirely outfitted before leaving the factory with furniture and fittings including flat-screen televisions, Nespresso™ coffee machine, and air conditioning. To move into a micro compact home, all you need is a toothbrush!

Nicole and Rupert will travel with the m-ch on a truck to Bremerhaven (on the north coast of Germany), where it will be loaded into a specially made sea container and then craned onto

Delivery of the micro compact home to the O₂ Village in 2005: two trucks were sufficient to transport the whole village of seven units with minimum distur-bance to the trees.

RG

JH

The micro com-pact home 007 is raised above the ground to enable a Smart™ car to be parked below

RH

the deck of a ship. The m-ch weighs 2.2 tons (less than a Bentley Continental, which weighs in at 2.4 tons), and can be lifted by helicopter to remote locations in the mountains, to islands or forests. The m-ch can also be delivered quickly for emergency accommodation. Once it arrives into the U.S. terminal in New York, it will be unloaded from the ship and loaded onto a truck for the journey to MoMA.

Nicole and Rupert will assemble and level the aluminium sub-frame onto the lot at MoMA and will prepare the utility connections. A light mobile crane will lift the m-ch into position. The legs of the frame can be adjusted to locate the m-ch on rough or sloping terrain and can be extended to enable the home to be situated on or at the water's edge or on flood plains. The micro compact home will be ready for use in less than two hours after it arrives off the truck at MoMA.

TW

TW

Model of the Tree Village: 30 micro compact homes with lift and stair access at the centre.

EO

appendix

MICRO COMPACT HOME: DESIGNED WITH STUDENTS FOR STUDENTS
by Richard Horden

blog nr. 5

In 2001, the teams in Munich were sharing ideas from Japan in weekly video conferences, and many different arrangements and experiments with the internal layout began to emerge.

Andreas Vogler and I had returned from Tokyo with a small 1:20 model showing the value of the recessed floor as in a Japanese tea house. This idea was quickly fed to the design teams as it removed the need for any chairs.

Students had to resolve the space into four simplified human functions – sleep, hygiene, food preparation and work. Storage had to serve each function, and all these functions were to be compacted into a 265cm cube.

Toilet and shower had to be combined into the same space and my experience of sailing in cruising yachts proved this. This 'hygiene/wet area' had to be at the front door to avoid clothes and shoes entering the living and bed space. A light sliding door conceals the wet area from the living. Most homes have a toilet close to the front door, but not all have a toilet IN the front entrance! I live and work in the micro compact home no. 007 in Munich and the position of the toilet is ideal. You are not aware of it when using the home, and it is 'out of sight and out of mind' in the concealed entrance lobby.

One important factor was constantly discussed ... the bed, should it fold away? I insisted that the bed space should be fixed and be visually separate from the work space. In Tokyo, I had been allocated a single room for visiting professors and I found that the most disturbing thing was to see the bed when you were trying to work and to see your work when you were trying to sleep!

It all sounds very simple and obvious now, with the micro compact home in constant use, but the configuration of the cube evolved from many 1:20 study models. By early 2002, we had 150 students building models and developing their own variants for the project. The final version of the micro compact home is the result of input from at least 200 students, 10 assistants, and 1 professor.

Most Institute parties then and now finish with groups squeezed into the first 'i-home' (now the micro compact home) 1:1 prototype in our studio. The m-ch is a 1.5-person home, so it is interesting to push the limit and see how many people we can fit into the home. So far, we've fit 14.

SK   WB

RH

The micro compact home and the Japanese tea house. Both are slightly raised above the ground and exist without the need for chairs and loose furniture.

DG

... Friday, 02 May 2008

LIVING IN THE M-CH
by Richard Horden

blog nr. 6

The *'Life in a Box'* movie was filmed and directed by Josh Cawthorn, Alfie Dale and Jim Petersen in 2008.

Every Monday morning for the past ten years I am happy to leave Heathrow Airport in the rain and fly into the sunlight with Swiss Airlines or Lufthansa to land at Europe's best airports – Zurich and Munich.

The experience and excellence of the in-flight design and crew presentation, designed by Strenesse, is a delight; but it is much more than that. It is also the inspiration for our projects, in particular the micro compact home... business class – short-stay smart living!

My stay in Munich lasts for only two nights (two and half working days). Following the 90-minute flight, I head to the University for meetings and lectures, and that evening I drive the Mercedes Smart™ (690cc/45 horsepower) to my micro compact home, which is waiting like a business-class seat to soften my day. I enjoy a short session on my laptop and a light, uncooked snack at the aluminium table below the soft white LED downlights (12 watts) and Swiss 'Zed light' (6 watts).

The students in nearby 'm-ch' 001-006 are barbecuing. They include Filipp and Kerstin, who has lived in 005 continuously since the opening in 2005. The smell of the charcoal smoke drifts through the slightly opened window of my 'm-ch'. I then catch a news update from BBC 24 or CNN on the flat-screen TV and soon am into the soft, plush, deep blue duvet on the eight foot by four foot, 1.5 person bed... the deep-toned, integral sound system plays Silje Nergaard.

At 06.15, the Braun alarm bleeps and I have a jog in the Englischer Garten, Munich's equivalent to London's Hyde Park. Twenty-six minutes later I am back at 'm-ch' 007 and the water heater has prepared the micro tank for precisely the amount of water I need for a hot shower — no more, no less. The Nespresso™ machine prepares a perfectly topped coffee served in a neat, pre-warmed Lufthansa Schoenwald cup. The spoon and dish with the *gipfeli* micro croissant, bought at Nah + Gut in Osterwaldstrasse at the turn point on my jog, are waiting on the now-daylight-washed workstation. I sketch my agenda for the day on the Swiss airline-format notepad and check that the battery on my Air Zermatt helicopter model is ready for the evening practice flight from 007. Later I will fly the Air Zermatt model across the freshly mowed lawn and between the tall lime trees.

I am fortunate to have such freedom to create and use a new model for living like the 'm-ch', and doubly fortunate to have the client, team of students, assistants, and charming family builders Gatterbauer (in London, Munich, and Uttendorf) to assist in bringing it to reality.

The micro compact home is a new model for a minimal, high-quality lifestyle, so personal it is tailored to my laptop and iPhone™, and so compact that my 10-inch diameter circular vacuum does not move as I clean the entire home with the 5-foot concertina tube.

I can customize the micro compact home with the latest Swiss airline brochure or a copy of Wallpaper opened at my favourite page. The high level of sound insulation and latest vacuum-thermal system cushion me from external sounds and temperature fluctuations. This is light, contemporary, personal living landed from 32,000 feet.

LUFTHANSA

SK

AV

LEARJET

MICRO COMPACT HOME AND THE AIRBUS A340
by Richard Horden

blog nr. 7

Andreas Sander-Carqueville is director of the pure white passenger terminals at Munich Airport and, thanks to him and his team, for the past 11 years we have been fortunate to be able to take our students on a tour of the entire airport.

Munich has been voted the best airport in Europe for five consecutive years; it is of great value to show our architectural students at the TU Munich.

In 2001 we made our July tour as usual and when inside the giant glass 300m-span (almost 1,000 feet) maintenance hangar we came across the crew rest cabin for the long-haul, four-engined Airbus A340, which was on a trolley in the hangar for maintenance.

This is basically a toughened air-freight container developed by Eurocopter to accommodate four to five crew beds for the alternative cabin crew on long-haul flights. The crew cabin is slid into the baggage hold area and has a ladder that connects it to the galley on the passenger floor above. Like the 'm-ch' today, it is built of aluminium with excellent task lighting, flat-screen information panels, and sound system to link the rest crew to the main deck. The internal height of the cabin is only 1.6m, similar to the seat areas at the window position in most aircraft. Bill Lear designed his celebrated sitting-only private jet in the fifties and was heavily criticized in the press for doing so. He replied that you cannot stand up in a Ferrari, either!

I was fascinated with the chance to make a sophisticated living 'cabin' using the same space, material, and weight-saving principles. Eurocopter was contacted by our team and information was gathered to inform and develop our project Tokyo 26/i-home design – later to become the micro compact home – and also for our other micro-architecture projects. We now focus on the standing and sitting-only areas in other projects in order to minimize material and land use, which also has the benefit of reducing carbon emissions in manufacture and costs and energy consumption during the project use. The design we are now developing at the University and the London office is called the 'family compact home', or the f-ch. This will also optimize space using the inspirational ideas of the Airbus crew rest cabin.

On Wednesday this week we will visit the 'm-ch' factory where the 'micro compact home' for MoMA is being completed and the installation of photovoltaic solar cells and wind turbine are being tested. In next week's blog I will explain the energy use and reduced carbon version of the 'm-ch'.

FM

LUFTHANSA

LUFTHANSA

RH

appendix

... *Friday, 16 May 2008*

MICRO COMPACT HOME:
CALM, LOW-MASS, LOW-ENERGY, LOW-MATERIAL USE.
by Richard Horden

blog nr. 8

Filipp Fuchs, one of the students who lives in a 'micro compact home' in Munich described how 'living in the "m-ch" takes something away from you – 'capacity' – and gives you something in return'. What does the 'm-ch' give in return?

Before moving in to the 'micro compact home' I had an apartment in a pleasant leafy part of Munich called Schwabing within a short walking distance from the University. It was a one-bedroom apartment of around 50m^2 (538 sq ft). It had a shiny parquet wood floor and white-painted plastered walls with the usual high-quality function and fittings you would expect in a Central European City. You could not criticize the apartment but it was a sad average sort of place, nothing special, no risk taking, no human scale and in fact I felt very alone there. I had no desire to personalize the space. It was more like a hotel room with a feeling that whatever I did to it would not affect its frigidity. I felt a cold distance to the place which provided the service without engagement, a totally sexless object!

The 'micro compact home' is a different issue; it is in fact an immaculately tailored series of small overlapping spaces. It has the comfort of a perfect suit, or an entirely state-of-the- art cockpit. A personally crafted place made with obvious loving care by a family builder and student design team. A calmness exists inside and embraces the user with its scale and subtle lighting. Every function has a perfectly scaled place; it feels an integral and complete part of modern life. You require little to personalize the space, a magazine, laptop or book open at the right page! Fully satisfied, I disposed of the 50m^2 in Schwabing for 6m^2 on The Englischer Garten.

I was to give a talk and TV interview at UBS in Zug in Switzerland in July 2006. The 'm-ch' was placed in the town square just outside the entrance to the bank and a television interviewer, Roland Blaser, commented in Swiss German 'Im "m-ch" fühlt man sich wie in einer Klosterzelle vom 21. Johrhundert, vernetzt mit der ganzen Welt', which translated as 'the

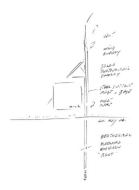

"m-ch" feels like a monk's cell for the 21st century networked to the whole world!'. I found this definition close to my personal experience with its almost religious sense of calm and yet its feeling of international connectivity. I put this down to the calm detailing. The strong use of horizontals, natural light carefully combined with LED downlights, and daylight side-wash illuminating all horizontal surfaces, the most calming of all lighting arrangements. Low mass, low energy and carbon neutral, the 'm-ch' weighs 2.3 tons. It is constructed using 0.5-inch ply on 4 x 2 timber framing with various finishes. The external skin is 3/32nd inch aluminium sheet; insulation is polyurethane foam with 1.5-inch vacuum insulation in the roof.The 'm-ch' uses 60 watts of energy for lighting with all of the LED downlights on. In addition I use three Swiss Zed lights, of 6 watts each, for enhanced task lighting. The fridge and freezer use 80 watts. The total continuous power use is around 160 watts with all lights on. In winter the 'm-ch' uses 348 kWhrs per month and in summer 123 kWhrs. [from 'm-ch' Full Life Cycle Analysis Report, by Zsuzsa Szalay / TU Munich] To run the 'm-ch' carbon neutrally it would require 8m^2 of solar cells working optimally at 100 watts per sqm at 5.33 hours per day in summer. Air conditioning requires 950 watts for intermittent use. In winter it would require 2.3 times that capacity to run the heating or the smallest wood-pellet stove available.

DG

TW

appendix

... Friday, 30 May 2008

MICRO COMPACT HOME : 'WINDOWS'
by Richard Horden

blog nr. 9

The Social window

Dieter Massberg is the Director of the Student Housing Authority in Munich, which has the largest student campus in Europe. His open and innovative character made the idea of building a student home from a 2.6m cube a reality. He had land available and had achieved some earlier innovations in housing. When I proposed the idea of the 2.6m cube to him he laughed and said 'we are definitely going to build this'. That was at the start of the teaching programme in October 2001; and when we discovered that we both shared a passion for Smart™ cars, that was the icing on the cube! Munich needs to accommodate 5,000 new students every year and, as there is a constant need for growth of the campus, there is room for exploring new ideas. Dieter was a regular visitor to the student presentations and always enthusiastic, polite, and positive.

The Technology window

A cube of 8 1/2 feet (2.6m) could have never worked as a practical home for students, or anyone else, before the invention of the internet, the laptop, the mobile phone, the flat-screen television, LED lighting, the microwave oven, and mini-bar fridge and freezer. Construction innovation had produced the 1 3/8 inch (3.5cm) vacuum insulation panel, which is the equivalent of approximately 3 15/16 inches (10cm) of polyurethane foam, and saves valuable space in the roof or wall composition. This was another product that was first commercially available in the new millennium. So a number of factors came together in 2001 to enable us to grasp the opportunity to design a sophisticated micro home for 'short stay smart living'. Students today can, but do not need to, buy quantities of books – the laptop is their library and is networked to the whole world. The design is like 'business class for students'.

The Art window

During the design development of the 'i-home/micro compact home', I had become increasingly skeptical about the four-legged support for the cube. A column under each corner of a cube destroys the purity of the form; the corners need to be kept clear. Artist Marijke de Goey and I worked for some time in Amsterdam and at the Poole house and what intrigued me was that her sculptures never had support on the corners. Like Alexander Calder and Kenneth Snelson, her sculptures rested on three supports, also a key principal of our micro-architecture projects. I changed the design of the 'm-ch' units for the O_2 village using three asymmetric points of support. This expressed the cubes with absolute clarity. We sketched ideas together and joined the micro compact home to her reed-like sculptures, and it sat like a bird's nest in the Dutch reeds. This had the effect of clarifying the cube form and expressing its verticality and connection to the land and nature in the form of the reed. We called the project the 'Reed Huis', in Dutch, *Riet Huis*. Marijke's father had worked for Gerrit Rietveld (*reitveld* means 'reed field'), a key architect member of the De Stijl movement with Mondrian and van Doesberg, and his 'art and architecture' house at Utrecht was our inspiration!

The Architecture window
We had been teaching micro architecture for five years at the TU Munich and the coaching team were now confident with the process and sequence and had built several micro-architecture projects with the students, like the Astronaut workstation for NASA (the seat restraint part designed by Hans Huber is now on the International Space Station) 'Cliffhanger' and 'Beach Point'. It was time to build a more ambitious and innovative urban, habitable micro architecture. The Technical Centre (student workshops with computer CNC machines at the TU Munich)had also just opened and we had all the technical help we needed to achieve a high-quality, large-scale prototype. Sponsorship from local Munich industries and the Bavarian State had also increased as a result of the success of these earlier projects. We had an excellent coaching team: Burkhard Franke, Lydia Haack, Walter Klasz, Hendrik Müller, Andreas Vogler and Tim Wessbecher, and enthusiastic client Dieter Massberg.

The Ecology window
Products were reducing in size (for example, Mercedes Smart™ appeared in the late 1990s) which made economic, ecological, and material sense, and we knew that this was the time to review the home in the same way, looking at 'the home as product design'. Our philosophy of 'touching the earth lightly' and 'less material more nature' fitted the drive to reduce carbon emissions in manufacture and minimize energy in use.

The 'O₂ Student Village' in Munich. The cubic forms, with all corners visible, contrast with the rich natural landscape.

RH   AMJ   EO   RH

MICRO COMPACT HOME: FROM STUDENT TO ARCHITECT, FROM CAMPUS TO CITY

by Richard Horden

blog nr. 10

Today the micro compact home is sailing to New York from somewhere off the British coast; the sea passage will take approximately seven days and there will be customs formalities of one week in New York docks before the truck delivery to MoMA on the 10th and 11th of June. One of the pleasures of teaching at the TU Munich has been to see the constant to and fro' of familiar smiling faces as young people move between the Institute and the London office. Having seen students for several semesters in studio it is a privilege for me to be able to offer them a short summer holiday job or sometimes permanent work placement in the office in central London. That way they move from one teaching environment to another! An office is also a learning environment, albeit a much tougher one where reality shifts to more demanding pressures on time, drawing accuracy and dimensional precision. I have great pleasure in handing some quite experienced young people to my partners Stephen Cherry and Billie Lee who then take on the guide role, and they are far happier to do this when they know that I have worked with those students for a few years.

For the student graduates there are advantages and familiarities. They have the same furniture system in the studio in Munich and the London office, System 26. They see and design projects which have some links to the work in Munich, and they have the input of colleagues whom they have known earlier at the University who can help with accommodation and with the shift from the clean 'alpine village' atmosphere of Munich to the fast, hard urban reality of London in 2008.

Campus and City

The micro compact home's unique quality is that it has been designed with and for young people. It has always been a dream of mine, a perfect scenario, to realize an urban village of micro compact homes in London where the young students from Munich or from English universities (such as Bath University with which we have an exchange programme) can move to for the first months of their stay in London or during short summer vacation jobs. The 'Tree Village' is a composition of 'micro compact homes' which I designed for both campus and city. Our office, when circumstances allow, plan to build a small cluster of micro compact homes in London for short-stay urban living.

Snowboard, Surfboard and Sports villages

The micro compact home can be built light enough, from 1.8 tons to 2.3 tons, to be installed by helicopter in the mountains or remote lakes or islands to enable young people and young-minded people to enjoy a close proximity to nature while being networked with excellent sound and visual systems.

micro compact home

Design team TU Munich: Vanessa Blacker-Sturm, Burkhard Franke, Victoria Gruber, Lydia Haack, Christian Hainzelmeier, Richard Horden, Walter Klasz, Stefan Koch, Bianca Matern, Hendrik Müller, Dietrich Oswald, Miroslav Penev, Wibke Seidler, Taissi Tuhkanen, Andreas Vogler, Tim Wessbecher
Client: O_2 Germany and Student Housing Authority Munich
Architectural team: Horden Cherry Lee, London, and Haack + Hopfner, Munich (O_2 Village)
Engineer : Tim Brengelmann
Graphics design: KMS Munich (O_2 Village), Ulrike Fuchs (book, brochure + exhibitions)
Contractor: Nicole and Rupert Gatterbauer, micro compact home Gmbh

EO   RH   RH   WK   TW

appendix

department tu munich
richard horden, univ. prof.

born	26 dec 1944
married to Kathy Horden	26 aug 1972
born	26 april 1946
died	26 oct 1998
two children	
Christian, born	19 nov 1985
Poppy, born	2 dec 1988

Schooling

Tremezzo Italy	1952
Perrot Hill and Bryanston	1953
Architectural Association	1963

Architectural Experience

Farrel Grimshaw	1971
Spence & Webster	1972
Foster Associates	1975
Richard Horden Associates	1985
Horden Cherry Lee	1998

Architectural Awards

Financial Times	1992
RIBA	1974/ 1993/2003
Civic Trust	1991/2001
BBC2	1994
Aluminium	1993/1997
building of the year	2003
and others	

various publications/international lectures/teaching and conferences	from 1974
Professor of Architecture and Product Design at Technical University, Munich	from 1996

SILVAPLANA 2006   UPF

acknowledgements

Alexandra von Petersdorff

Burkhard Franke, Wiss. Ass.

Hendrik Müller, Wiss. Ass.

Nadine Zinser, Wiss. Ass.

Wieland Schmidt, Wiss. Ass.

Walter Klasz, Wiss. Ass.

Ulrike Fuchs, Wiss. Ass.

Tim Wessbecher, Wiss. Ass.

Hans Huber

Both architecture and teaching involve teamwork, and one of the many pleasures of the Institute in Munich has been the drive for high quality combined with the always polite and caring nature of the assistants and 'hiwi' student assistants.

The constant flow of bureaucracy, financial planning and personal care for the students is managed by my very efficient and reliable secretary Alexandra von Petersdorff.

The teaching assistants on the left are all qualified architects and many are experienced mountaineers, such as Tim Wessbecher and Walter Klasz, who also made a famous rescue of his professor from 3,890m in May 2004. Burkhard Franke manages the lectures on building typology and organizes our design workshops. Others have interests in horse riding and art, Ulrike Fuchs and many others ski and sail on the beautiful mountains and lakes close to the city. The quality of environment and teamwork are an essential combination in the micro-architecture workshops.

appendix

department tu munich
assistants

Burkhard Franke, Dipl.Ing., Architect

2008/	freelancer at *Detail* magazine
2002/	own practice in Munich
	> www.burkhard-franke.de
2002/08	teaching + research dep. of Prof. Horden, TU Munich
2000/02	Lauber Architects, Munich
1998/00	Canali/Botti Architects, Munich
1997/98	diploma at TU-Stuttgart
1996/97	DAAD scholarship, studies at ASU Phoenix
	Design Excellence Award
1991/96	studies at TU Stuttgart
1988/91	training as carpenter
1967	born in Regensburg/Germany

Hans Huber, Dipl.-Ing., Architect

2000/	teacher for 'Architecture in space and extreme environment', Dept. of Prof. Horden, TU-Munich, founding of Huber Matzenau GmbH
1999	Coordinator of space project, Dept. of Prof. Horden, TU-Munich
1998	consultant at Dept. of Prof. Horden, TU-Munich
1988	own office in Landsberg
1987	office of Prof. Schuck, Munich
1987	diploma at TU-Munich
1960	born in Landshut/Germany

Wieland Schmidt, Dipl.Ing., Architect

2005/	own practice in Munich
	> www.wieland-schmidt-architeken.de
2005/	teaching + research Dept. of Prof. Horden, TU Munich
2001/05	Helmut Jahn, Chicago
2001	Werner Sobek, Stuttgart
2001	diploma at TU-Stuttgart
1999/00	student research assistant, Inst. for lightweight structures
1998/01	studied at TU Stuttgart
1997/98	studied at TU Vienna
1995/97	studied at Univ. Kaiserslautern
1973	born in Berlin/Germany

Tim Wessbecher, Dipl. Ing. FH, Architect

2006/	own practice in Munich
	> www.tntarchitektur.de
2003/	teaching + research Dept. of Prof. Horden, TU Munich
2001	Haack+Höpfner Architects, Munich
2000	diploma FH-Karlsruhe
1995	practice in different offices: PIA-Architects, Prof. G. Gassmann, Speicher+Partner
1995	studies at FH-Karlsruhe
1993	internship at Baltin+Partner
1987	training as mechanic
1970	born in Rastatt/Germany

Hendrik Müller, Dipl. Ing.

2006/	member of scientific committee, edA–esempi di Architettura/Italy
2005/	own practice in Munich eins:33 Architecture & Interior Design > www.einszu33.de
2001	teaching + research Dep. of Prof. Horden,TU Munich diploma, Cultural Center Atrani, Amalfi / Italy
1999	co-founder of eins:33, Stuttgart
1998	intern studio uda, Torino/Italy
1994/01	studied Architecture & Design, Staatliche Akademie der Bildenden Künste, Stuttgart
1973	born in Böblingen/Germany

Nadine Zinser, Dipl. Ing., Architect

2007/	own practice in Munich
2005/	teaching + research Dept. of Prof. Horden, TU Munich
2004/05	Olga Subirós, cloud9, Barcelona
2004	Daniel Modól de Tell, Barcelona
2003	Alfredo Arribas, Barcelona
2003	diploma at TU Stuttgart
2002	MGT Architects, Sydney
2001	studied at Accademia di Architettura, Mendrisio
1997/00	studied at TU Stuttgart
1977	born in Freudenstadt/Germany

Walter Klasz, Dipl. Ing., Architect

2008/09	guest professor at the university of applied sciences Giessen
2003/	own praxis in Innsbruck > www.klasz.at
2002/	teaching + research dep. of Prof. Horden,TU Munich
2001/02	project manager for the company Kusolitsch ray1 by Delugan_Meissl, Vienna
2001	diploma at TU Vienna: 1:1 built patented project
1998/01	Kronreif & partner, Vienna
1994/97	studies at the TU Vienna and ETSA-Sevilla
1993	internship as a carpenter in Argentina
1975	born in Vienna/Austria

Ulrike Fuchs, Dipl. Ing., Architect

2008/	teaching + research dept. of Prof. Horden, TU Munich
2005/08	Horden Cherry Lee Architects, London
2005	diploma at TU Munich
2003	Ackermann und Partner, Munich
2002/04	Kochta Architekten, Munich
2002/05	studies at TU Munich
2000/02	studies at TU Cottbus
1979	born in Munich/Germany

appendix

department tu munich
former assistants

Andreas Vogler, Dipl. Arch. ETH., Architect

2003/	foundation of 'Architecture and Vision' with Arturo Vittori specializing on aerospace architecture, technology transfer and mobile buildings **>** www.architectureandvision.com
2003/04	visiting professor at Royal Academy of Arts in Copenhagen
1997/00	several prize winning competitions with Thomas Straub
1996/02	teaching + research Dep. of Prof. Horden, TU Munich
1995/96	associate at Richard Horden Associates
1988/94	studies at ETH and RISD, USA
1986/88	pract. training interior design
1984/86	studies art history and literature Univ. Basle, TU Berlin
1964	born in Basle

Lydia Haack, Dipl. Ing., Architect

1996/04	teaching + research Dept. of Prof. Horden, TU Munich
1995/	office with John Höpfner **>** www.haackhoepfner.com various publications, lectures teaching at TU Munich
1991/95	M. Hopkins + Partners, London
1989/91	DAAD Scholarship, studies at the AA, London, AA diploma
1988	diploma at FH Munich
1965	born in Hof/Germany

Prof. Christian Kern, Dipl. Ing., Architekt

2007/	Prof. for three-dimensional design at TU Vienna
2001/	partner at Blauwerk architects, Munich **>** www.blauwerk.info
1999/04	teaching + research dept. of Prof. Horden, TU Munich
1989/95	different offices: Stirling+Wilford / Ken Yeang, Behnisch / Auer+Weber / MSP
1995	diploma at TU Stuttgart
1994	studies at Curtain University, Perth
1984/86	training as a mechanician
1964	born in Wipperfürth/Germany

Siegfried Lichtenauer
Eva Neumeyer
Claudia Pöppel
Michael Schneider
Leslie Stein
Thomas Straub
Craig Synnestvedt

department tu munich
administration

Technical University Munich
Faculty for Architecture

Institute for Architecture and Product Design
Univ. Prof. Richard Horden
Arcisstr. 21
80333 Munich
Germany

phone: +49 (0)89.289 22 491
fax: +49 (0)89.289 28 408

www.light.ar.tum.de

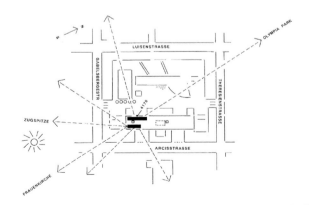

credits

Photography

Luciano D'Angelo	L D'A
Allianz Arena | B. Ducke	Allianz Arena | B. Ducke
British Aerospace	BAe
Doug Allan	The Image Bank | Getty Images
Eclipse Aviation Corporation	Eclipse Aviation Corporation
Bill Bachman	BB
Boat International	BI
Werner Blaser	WB
Carlo Borlenghi	CB
Ken Boyd	KB
BMW	BMW
David Carnwarth	DC
Edvard Cernoch	EC
Stephen Cherry	SC
Le Corbusier	LC
Art Davis	AD
Richard Davis	RD
John Donat	JD
Doppelmayr	Doppelmayr
Mira Esposito	ME
Florian Fischötter	FF
Burkhard Franke	BF
Ulrike Fuchs	UF
Virgin Gallactic	VIRGIN GALACTIC
Rupert Gatterbauer	RG
Dennis Gilbert	DG
Frank Greenaway	Dorling Kindersley | Getty Images
Hans Grossen	HG
Hiroshi Hamaya	HH
Hayes Davidson	HD
Coop Himmelb(l)au	CHb
Ruedi Homberger	Ho
John Hopfner	JH
Richard Horden	RH
Russell Jones	RJ
Arnold M. Jansan	AMJ
Alex Kallenberger	AK
Jan Kaplicky	JK
Elsworth Kelly	EK
Ken Kirkwood	KK
Walter Klasz	WK
Tom Körber	TK
Learjet	Learjet
Sascha Kletzsch	SK
Steffen Knopp	SKn
Lord Lichfield	PL
Andrea Leiber	AL
Loungepark	Stone | Getty Images
Lufthansa	Lufthansa
Eastcott Momatiuk	Eastcott Momatiuk
Hendrik Müller	HM
Inga Mannewitz	IM
Safer Motherhood	SM
Nasa	NASA
Foster + Partners	FP
Max Prugger	MP
Gilberto Penzo	GP
Ulrich Pfammatter	U Pf
Porsche	PORSCHE
Giles Martin-Raget	GM-R
Meer & Yachten	MY
Technical University Munich	TUM
Tom Miller	TM
Eamon O'Mahoney	EO
Ph. Toni Meneguzzo	Ph. Toni Meneguzzo
Armando Salas Portugal	ASP
Alexandra v. Petersdorff	AvP
Porsche	PORSCHE
Christina Reschke	TR
Sandra Spindler	SSp
D. Shaw-Ashton	DS-A
Wieland Schmidt	WS
Ermin Smrekar	ES
Kilian Schuster	KS
Peter Stumpf	PS
Swiss	SWISS
Jørn Utzon	JU
Andreas Vogler	AV
Robin Webster	RW
Tim Wessbecher	TW
Alfred Wolf	AW
Konrad Wothe	Minden Pictures | Getty Images

Wally
Nadine Zinser

WALLY
NZ

Models

Amalgam
Unit 22 In London
Tim Wessbecher and Students at the TU Munich

Project Credits

Courtyard House
1974
Richard Horden

Sainsbury Centre For Visual Arts
1978
Work For Norman Foster

Yacht House
1983
Richard Horden, Peter Horden

Geodetic Balloons
1986
Kathy Horden, Richard Horden, Tony Hunt, Robin
Webster

Aerospace Table
1989
Mira Esposito, Richard Horden, Sarah Kirby, Billie
Lee

Graphite Chair
1989
Mira Esposito, Richard Horden, Sarah Kirby, Billie
Lee

Flying Water
1990
Ken Boyd, Richard Horden, Sarah Kirby, Brian Kelly

Skydeck House
1990
Richard Horden, Thomas Höger, Sarah Kirby, Oliver
Stirling, Michael Wigginton

Smart™ Car House
2000
Richard Horden, Omar Guebel, Manuel Pittino,
Stefan Scholz

Ski Haus
1991
Ken Boyd, Richard Horden, Sarah Kirby, Brian Kelly

Aeros Door Handle
1992
Richard Horden, Sarah Kirby, Billie Lee

K1
1993
Klaus Daniels, John Donat, Peter Heppel, Ludwig
Ilg, Richard Horden, Sarah Kirby, Andreas Vogler

Swiss-Air Tower
1993
Sarah Forbes Waller, Richard Horden, Sarah Kirby,
Sarah North

Queen's Stand
1993
Claire Cheney, Sarah Forbes Waller, Alan Grant,
Richard Horden, Caroline Hislop, Thomas Höger,
Russell Jones, Sarah Kirby, Silke Krüger, Billie Lee,
Eva Martin, Brian McClymont, Susan McClean,
Dominic Reid, Martina Sedelmayer, Js, Oliver
Stirling, Josh Wilson, Michael Wigginton

Point Lookout
1993
Sarah Forbes Waller, Russell Jones, Richard
Horden, Sarah Kirby

appendix

credits

Folding Canopies
1994
Mira Esposito, Sarah Forbes Waller, Richard Horden,
Brian Kelly, Billie Lee, Sarah North

Fish Haus
1996
Gerhard Abel, Willi Frötschner, Ursula Hammerschick,
Silvia Hörndl, Richard Horden, Martin Janecek, Brigitta
Kunsch, Paul Linsbauer, Christopher Lottersberger,
Michael Quixtner, Magrit Rammer, Hannes Schillinger,
Andreas Vogler, Anne Wagner, Sakura Watanabe

Beach Point
1997
Lydia Haack, Richard Horden, Markus Kottermair,
Jürgen Schubert, Thorsten Schwabe, Peter Zimmer

Kayak Club
1997
Jean-Paul Amato, Richard Horden, Johannes Talhof,
Andreas Vogler

Cliffhanger
1997
Alexander Felix, Richard Horden, Christopher von der
Howen, Eva Neumeyer, Andreas Vogler

Silva Spider
1997
Jürgen Amann, Rainer Barthel, Tim Brengelmann,
Richard Horden, Thomas Wenig, Andreas Vogler

Tree Tent
1997/1998
Ralf Drewing, Richard Horden, Petra Liedl, Claudia
Pöppel, Richard Schindler, Markus Vogl

Modular Display System
1997/1998
Lydia Haack, Michaela Hoppe, Richard Horden,
Christopher von der Howen, Eva Neumeyer,
Andreas Vogler, Markus Möslein, Peter Trunzer, Alu
Meier, Bartenbach Lichtlabor Gmbh Microgravity

Projects – International Space Station
1998/2004
Constance Adams, Bianca Artopé, Horst Baier,
Björn Bertheau, Brigitte Borst, Heiner Bubb,
Thomas Dirlich, Reinhold Ewald, David Fitts,
Julia Habel, Lydia Haack, H. Hamacher, Claudia
Hertrich, Alexander Hoffmann, Sandra Hoffmann,
Christian Hooff, Richard Horden, Hans Huber,
Eduard Igenbergs, Arne Laub, Nathan Moore,
Ernst K. Pfeiffer, Claudia Pöppel, David Ray,
Andreas, Vogler, Alu Meier, Bayern Innovativ, Bund
Der Freunde Der TU-München, Brück Leichtbau-
technik, Hans Grohe, Horbach Werbetechnik,
Käthe Kruse, Oererckenschwig, Rosner Lacke,
Schreinerei Gleissner & Stevens, Specken Drumag,
Vontana Wasserbetten

Tensegrity Bridge
1998
Søren Aagaard, Susy Carolin Baasel, Gudrun
Holzer, Richard Horden, Ng Gin Ling,
Karin Skousbøll, Andreas Vogler, Michael Woodford

White Water
1998
Rainer Barthel, Tim Brengelmann, Katrin Doll,
Sabine Frohmader, Richard Horden, Christina
Reschke, Craig Synnestvedt, Claudia Wieshuber

Air Camp
1998
Julia Haas, Richard Horden, Andreas Kienle,
Eva Neumeyer, Andreas Vogler

City Arcade
1999
Stefano Angaroni, Stephen Cherry, Adrian Fowler,
Davis Franklin, Richard Horden, Billie Lee, Peter
Ludwig, Kwamina Monney, Jurgan Schubert, Andreas
Vogler, Danielle Williams, Peter Zimmer

Astronaut Workstation
2000
Björn Bertheau, Lydia Haack, Claudia Hertrich, Richard
Horden, Hans Huber, Arne Laub, Claudia Pöppel,
Andreas Vogler

Space Shower
2000
Bianca Artopé, Brigitte Borst, Lydia Haack, Richard
Horden, Hans Huber, Claudia Pöppel, Andreas Vogler

Wing Tower
2001
Peter Heppel, Richard Horden, Billie Lee

Light Harp
2001
Lavinia Herzog, Richard Horden, Thomas Straub

One Kilo House
2001
Richard Horden, Tillmann Kühnel, Moritz Mungenast,
Klaus Puchta, Thomas Straub

Carbon Fibre House
2001
Lydia Haack, Richard Horden, Christian Kern, Matthias
Pektor, Christoph Röttinger, Michael Schneider

Camera House
2001
Kerstin Engelhardt, Richard Horden,
Torsten Schlauersbach, Thomas Straub

Fly Off
2001/2002
Clemens Bachmann, Richard Horden, Michael Stoppe

Ercol Furniture Factory
2002
Stephen Blowers, Stephen Cherry, David Franklin,
Pascal Gysi, Rainer Hofmann, Richard Horden, Billie
Lee, Peter Ludwig, Kwamina Monney, Manon Stock-
hammer

House On Evening Hill
2002
Mira Esposito, Richard Horden, Sarah Kirby

Reed Huis
2002
Marijke de Goey, Lydia Haack, Richard Horden

i-Home
2002
Vanessa Blacker-Sturm, Burkhard Franke, Veronika
Gruber, Lydia Haack, Claus Hainzlmeier, Richard
Horden, Walter Klasz, Stephan Koch, Bianca Matern,
Hendrik Müller, Daniel Oswald, Miroslav Penev, Wiebke
Seidler, Taisi Tuhkanen, Tim Wessbecher

Dubai Souq Bridge
2002
Sabine Kunzfeld, Richard Horden, Jacob Plötz,
Andreas Vogler

Seagull Bridge
2002
Burkhard Franke, Georg Glas, Julian Hildebrand,
Richard Horden

Auberge Du Verdon
2002
Richard Horden, Birgitta Kunsch, Frieder Lohmann,
Tobias Mattes

credits

Peak Lab 2
2002/2003
Peter Böhm, Ulrike Fuchs, Lydia Haack, Richard
Horden, Walter Klasz, Christian Neubauer, Michael
Smola, Andreas Orgler

Desert Flight
2002/2003
Matthäus Deffner, Lydia Haack, Christian Heck,
Richard Horden, Albert Pernpeintner

M-Igloo
2003
Ilona Gallitzdörfer, Lydia Haack, Richard Horden,
Christine Müller

Peak Lab
2003
Christoph Baumann, Vitus Erni, Christian Fierz,
Burkhard Franke, Matthias Frey, Yann Friedl, Stefan
Gassmann, Felix Häusler, Christian Heck, Lydia Haack,
Richard Horden, Walter Klasz, Christine Neumann,
Ulrich Pfammatter, Iwan Plüss, Daniel Schatzmann,
Christian Schmidiger, David Schneeberger, Urs
Schürch, Florian Uhl

Loch Ness Museum
2003
Burkhard Franke, Richard Horden, Walter Klasz,
Stoyan Todorov

Euro Tower
2003/2004
Rainer Barthel, Ulrich Egger, Burkhard Franke, Georg
Glas, Julian Hildebrand, Richard Horden, Fabian
Matthes, Albert Pernpeintner, Georg Rötzel, Minh N.
Thai, Stefan Winter

European Expo Tower
2003/2004
Rainer Barthel, Burkhard Franke, Fabian Gärtner,
Richard Horden, Albert Pernpeintner, Christian von

Sieg, Vitus Straehuber, Rodrigo Uzquiano, Andreas Walther,
Arndt Weiss, Stefan Winter

Serenissima
2003/2004
Burkhard Franke, Lydia Hack, Eva-Maria Hopper, Richard
Horden, Sidonie Kade

Summer Art School
2003/2004
Francesca Depol, Richard Horden, Christian Kern, Alexander Remke, Hannah Schubert

System 26 Furniture System
2004
Fabiana Chirivi, Richard Horden, Florian Rist, Tim
Wessbecher

Twisty Table
2004
Richard Horden, Werner Olschock, Tim Wessbecher

m-ch
2005
The m-ch was developed at the Technical University
Munich at the Institute for Architecture and Product Design
under Prof. Richard Horden with his teaching assistants
and students V. Blacker-Sturm, B. Franke, V. Gruber,
L. Haack, C. Hainzlmeier, R. Horden, W. Klasz, S. Koch,
B. Matern, H. Müller, D. Oswald, M. Penev, W. Seidler,
T. Tuhkanen, A. Vogler, T. Wessbecher.
The micro compact home design is the copyright
of Richard Horden. All rights reserved.
micro compact home ltd., Tel 00 44 207 495 4119
Architects: Horden Cherry Lee, London
Haack + Höpfner Munich, Tel 00 49 89 1239 1731
Production: m-ch micro compact home production Gmbh,
Uttendorf, Austria, Tel 00 43 7724 619720
Concept and Development: TU Munich, Institute Prof.
Richard Horden
European and USA Patents: Richard Horden

Spiral Lab
2004
Burkhard Franke, Marijke de Goey, Caroline
Haberkorn, Richard Horden, Werner Olschok,
Christine Schmidt, Tim Wessbecher

Polar Lab
2005
Simone Hiesinger, Richard Horden, Michael Kehr,
Eike Schling, Wieland Schmidt, Sandra Spindler

Ice Station
2005
Simone Hiesinger, Richard Horden, Wieland
Schmidt, Sandra Spindler

Event Centre Silvaplana 1
2005/2006
Ulrich Pfammatter, Richard Horden, Cajetan Piaget,
Henry Rist, Wieland Schmidt, Sebastian Uhl, Fabio
Wendnagel

Event Centre Silvaplana 2
2005/2006
Jérome Anton, Richard Horden, Walter Klasz,
Annegret Lochbrunner, Ulrich Pfammatter, Cajetan
Piaget, Daniel Castilla Toledo, Nadine Zinser

TU_FiN
2006
Stefan Ballmeier, Marisa Dressler, Kirstin Eichelberg,
Martin Francis, Richard Horden, Ivan Kiryakov,
Gilberto Penzo, Nadine Zinser

Solar Proa
2006
Tibor Bartholomä, Daniel Boos, Carolin Dißmann,
Martin Francis, Richard Horden, Gilberto Penzo,
Wieland Schmidt, Andreas Schwab

'iPod'™ House
2006/2007
Florian Dressler, Richard Horden, Nadine Zinser

Drift
2006/2007
Roy Fleetwood, Burkhard Franke, Richard Horden,
Annalena Priester, Benjamin Rantz, Lisa-Maria Thaler

New Zealand Out-Bach
2006/2007
Roy Fleetwood, Burkhard Franke, Tristan Franke, Daniel
Haimerl, Richard Horden, Valton Limani, Simone Mans, Tina
Rau, Julia Wolf, Nadine Zinser

Point Penguin
2006/2007
Richard Horden, Juae Kim, Walter Klasz, Guido Kleffel,
Wieland Schmidt

Rts
2006/2007
Florian Brummann, Peter Holzner, Richard Horden, Guido
Kleffel, Nadine Zinser

Tripolar
2006/2007
Guido Kleffel, Richard Horden, Robin Renner, Wieland
Schmidt, Simon Vorhammer

Desert Lodge
2007
Burkhard Franke, Richard Horden, Na Shen, Karin Wouters

Cocoon
2007
Burkhard Franke, Richard Horden, Andreas Schwab,
Marius Timmermann

appendix

credits

cc/001
2007
Richard Horden, Tim Wessbecher

Solar Pebble
2007/2008
Burkhard Franke, Simon Frick, Richard Horden,
Katharina Kassner

Solar Compact Home
2007/2008
Tjark-Marten Apetz, Philipp Groh, Richard Horden

Family Compact Home 01
2008
Richard Horden, Tim Wessbecher

Family Compact Home 02
2008
Burkhard Franke, Simon Frick, Richard Horden,
Katharina Kassner

Family Compact Home 03
2008, in progress
Anna Baumgartner, Birgit Neulinger, Richard Horden,
Walter Klasz

credits

Consultants

Constance Adams
AYH Partnership
Prof. Horst Baier
Bartenbach Lichtlabor Gmbh
Prof. Rainer Barthel
Werner Blaser
Tim Brengelmann
Prof. Heiner Bubb
David Chipperfield
Prof. Klaus Daniels
Dalton Warner Davies
Francesca Depol
East London University
Elisabeth Endres
Oscar Faber
Prof. Roy Fleetwood
Marino Folin
Sir Norman Foster
Freud Lemos Ltd.
Richard Freuer
Martin Francis
Marijke de Goey
Dyfed Griffiths
Lydia Haack
Prof. Gerhard Hausladen
HL Technik
John Höpfner
Kathy Horden
Richard Horden
Tony Hunt
Jan Kaplicky
Guido Kleffel
Prof. Boris Laschka
MACE Ltd.
Jem Main
Clyde Malby
Werner Olschok
Andreas Orgler

Gilberto Penzo
Prof. Albert Pernpeintner
Prof. Ulrich Pfammatter
Cajetan Piaget
Heinz Richter
Prof. Helmut Richter
Prof. Urs Rieder
Dirk Schmauser
Prof. Joseph Schwartz
Walter Schwaiger
UnternehmerTUM
Vilsmayer Metallbau
Andreas Vogler
Philipp Weber
Robin Webster
Tim Wessbecher
Prof. Stefan Winter

appendix

Ulrike Fuchs with the 'NZ' bridge model, London 2008

appendix

A special thank you to Ulrike Fuchs for her hard work and excellent design direction in achieving this book in such a compact time from March to June 2008, to get it ready for the exhibition of the micro compact home at the Museum of Modern Art. Ulrike also directed the micro compact home brochures from 2006 to 2008 during her very supportive work in our London office.

To Phyllis Richardson for her foreword and for her rapid text checking.

Thank you

ZH 462 897 at Air Glaciers, Lauterbrunnen, CH